GRANNY SQUARE FASHION

Master one granny square:
create 15 different stylish looks

CASSIE WARD

Search Press

Contents

GRANNY SQUARE
FASHION

Published in 2024 by
Search Press Ltd
Wellwood
North Farm Rd
Tunbridge Wells
Kent TN2 3DR

Reprinted 2024

ISBN-13: 978-1-80092-225-9
ebook ISBN: 978-1-80093-207-4

QUAR. 1169714

Conceived, edited and designed by
Quarto Publishing, an imprint of The Quarto Group
1 Triptych Place, London, SE1 9SH

Pattern checker: Rachel Vowles
Copy editor: Lindsay Kauber
Illustrator: Olya Kamieshkova and Kang Kuo Chen
Cover and layout designer: Sally Bond
Editor: Charlene Fernandes
Art director: Martina Calvio
Designer: Eliana Holder
Editorial Assistant: Elinor Ward
Photographer: Leanne Jade
Stylist: Claire Montgomerie
Make-up artist: Julia Edwards
Publisher: Lorraine Dickey

Bookmarked Hub
For further ideas and inspiration,
and to join our free online community,
visit www.bookmarkedhub.com

Printed in China

40

Beach Day Headband

44

Abstract Squares Tank Top

52

Bright & Breezy Tote Bag

58

Carnival Cowl

64

Sixties-Style Mini Dress

72

Half & Half Jumper

80

Summer Nights Wrap

86

Kaleidoscope Jumper

94

Retro T-shirt

102

Cozy Cropped Cardigan

110

Boho-Chic Maxi Waistcoat

118

Everyday Long Cardigan

About this Book

This book is a wonderful resource of fashion-led, granny square projects. Once you have mastered the classic granny square, you can then make a whole range of larger projects, such as a jumper, by joining multiple squares. The best part of making your own clothes and accessories is the chance to choose yarns and colours you love – or you can use the ones I've suggested in this book – it's up to you!

The Granny Square (pages 12–19)

You will find information on creating the basic granny square and the different variations.

The Projects (pages 20–125)

At the heart of this book are the 15 projects, including the Boho-Chic Maxi Waistcoat shown below. Clearly written patterns, stitch diagrams and inspiring photographs take you through each design – all you need to get started.

Skill level gives a guide to difficulty: easy, intermediate or advanced.

A close-up of a granny square from the project is shown here so you can see the details.

The colours and quantities of yarn needed to make the square are listed, along with any other materials needed and page references to relevant granny charts. Yarn quantities alter for different sizes. This is shown in brackets. Read more about yarn quantities on page 139.

This panel is a visual representation of the colours used in the project. However, you can use any colour combination you want for your own project.

Photos of the garment or accessory are shown in full and at different angles.

Full colour schematics are provided for each project, which indicate the placement of the squares and where to join them. The finished size of the project is also shown here.

A written pattern takes you through the pattern round by round or row by row.

The techniques section on pages 126–141 will explain each stitch in more detail if you are new to crochet or need a refresher.

The finished square size is shown here along with information on tension. The finished square size will change for the different garment sizes. This is shown in brackets. Learn more about sizing on page 139.

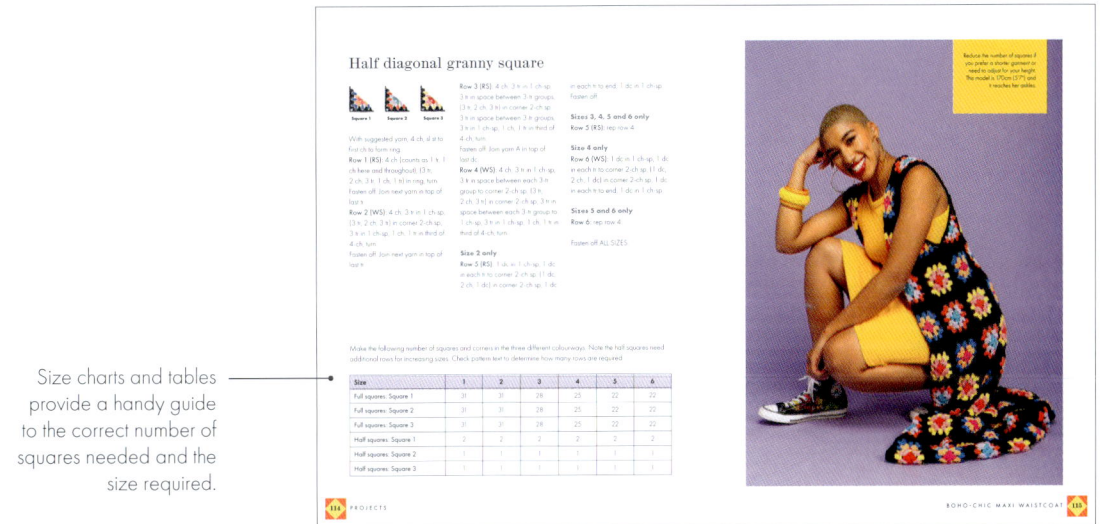

Size charts and tables provide a handy guide to the correct number of squares needed and the size required.

Stitches and Techniques (pages 126–141)

This section provides information on how to read patterns and charts; the tools and materials required; and crochet stitches and techniques.

Meet Cassie

As a child, I was always creative. I could draw, paint, sew, knit and embroider. My great aunt Alice was an avid crocheter and I longed to be able to do what she did. I'm left-handed and after many unsuccessful attempts to teach me, she finally gave up on me.

After losing my dear mum, Josie, in my late 20s, I suffered terribly with anxiety and needed a distraction from my overactive mind. I was at an exhibition sitting next to an Irish lady from the UK Hand Knitting Association. I picked up a hook, she taught me the basics of crochet there and then, and sent me on my way. I was instantly addicted and began designing immediately.

I made amazing creations, but never having learned how to read a pattern, I had no real idea of what stitches I was using! I needed proper lessons. A lovely lady named Helen taught me how to read patterns and showed me new techniques. From this, The Missing Yarn, my crochet business, was born.

When I'm not crocheting, I'm a single mum to the most amazing identical twin boys. We live in a sleepy English village in Cambridgeshire and my twins' drive and determination to succeed amazes me on a daily basis. I'm so proud of the young men they are becoming. I sadly lost my dad this year to pancreatic cancer – he was my biggest supporter when it came to crochet and I definitely miss him cheering me on.

I love playing with different stitches, styles and textures. Many of my designs are inspired by my love of fashion and a desire to be different. The designs in this book are derived from my love of abstract art and its vivid shapes and colours, so the palette I've chosen is bold, bright and cheerful.

This book is an absolute dream come true and I'm so thankful for the opportunity to share my designs with you. I love the humble granny square and I am always astonished at the diverse range of things that can be made with them.

I hope the book will inspire you to make some beautiful, unique crochet items, and that you get the same amount of joy from making them as I did from writing them.

Cassie xxx

P.S. Share your projects on social media with the tag #GrannySquaresWithCassie and tag me @themissingyarn. You can also find more of my patterns at www.themissingyarn.co.uk

CHAPTER ONE:

The Granny Square

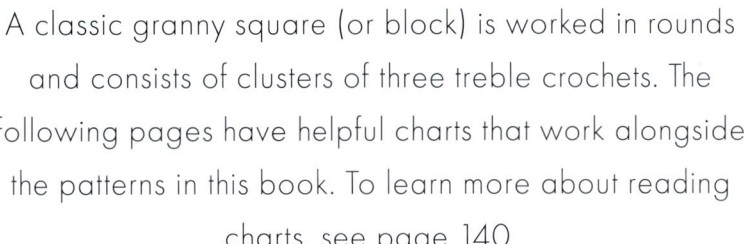

A classic granny square (or block) is worked in rounds and consists of clusters of three treble crochets. The following pages have helpful charts that work alongside the patterns in this book. To learn more about reading charts, see page 140.

This chart is only shown to the end of round 6.

Key

⬭ ch

† tr

• sl st

► beginning of round

The Classic Granny

If you prefer using a chart alongside a pattern, then this chart will be useful in creating the classic granny square, which is used for the majority of the projects. However, please refer to the written pattern, as each project will have a different number of rounds.

- Granny squares are created with groups of treble crochet stitches and chain stitches.

- The beginning ring can either be a magic ring or a foundation ring (see page 131).

- Each round starts with a chain three. This counts as your first treble crochet, however, the pattern will always make this clear.

- The classic granny square joins a new colour at each round, so no two rounds are the same. If you want to work your square in one colour only, see pages 16–17.

- All of the stitches on a granny square are worked into the spaces between the 3-tr groups made on the previous round and into the 2-ch sp at each corner.

- Extra stitches and chains form the corners.

- Just remember the principle of 3 tr, 2 ch, 3 tr in each corner ch-2 space, and 3 tr in each space between 3-tr groups until next corner.

Projects

- Rainbow Shopper
- Mix & Match Bucket Hat
- Floral Headscarf
- Beach Day Headband
- Abstract Squares Tank Top
  (note that round 5 uses double crochet edging).
- Bright and Breezy Beach Bag
- Carnival Cowl
- Sixties-Style Mini Dress
- Half & Half Jumper
- Summer Nights Wrap
- Kaleidoscope Jumper
- Retro T-shirt
- Cozy Cropped Cardigan
- Boho-Chic Maxi Waistcoat
- Everyday Long Cardigan

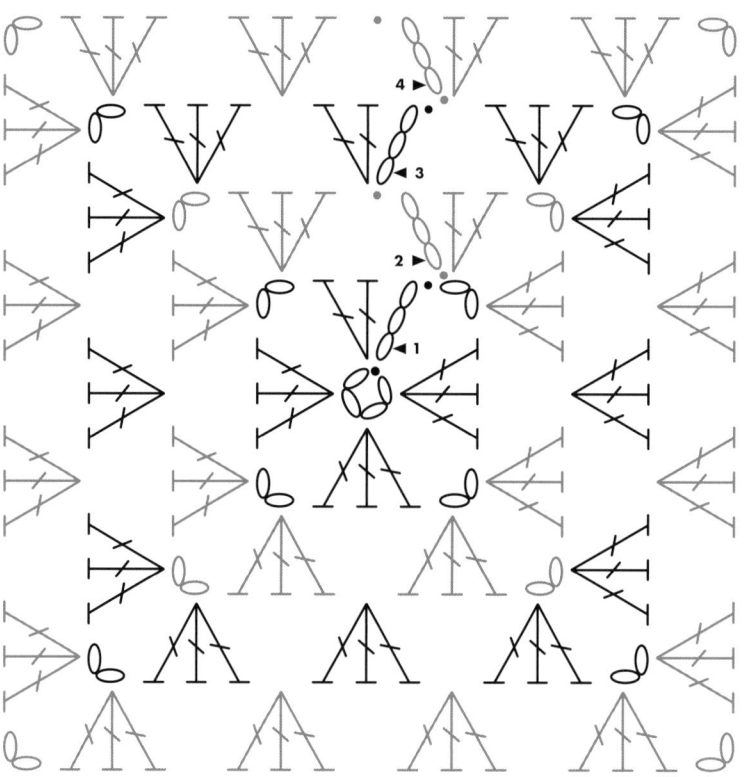

This chart is only shown to the end of round 4.

Key

○ ch

┤ tr

• sl st

► beginning of round

The Turned Granny

The turned granny, or the one-colour granny, looks almost the same as the classic granny. The only difference is that you do not have to change colours.

- When making the classic granny, you begin each round in a different space to the previous round because you join in a new colour. The turned granny chart shows a slip stitch and the round starting directly above the start of the previous round because you do not change the colour.

- Although there is only one project in this book that follows this chart, it is the easiest way to make a granny square and will result in only two ends to weave in!

Projects

- Sixties-Style Mini Dress (note that round 5 does join in a new colour as a border).

GRANNY SQUARE TIPS

- There are two ways of creating granny squares: some crochet designers prefer to add chain stitches between the 3-tr groups and some work straight into the next space created by the 3-tr group. If you add the chain stitches in between, it will make your granny square bigger than intended for the patterns in this book.

- All of the projects require multiple granny squares. Once you have created your first granny square and checked the tension, it might be easier to make the remaining granny squares, round by round (that is, create only round one for all remaining squares). Then round two in your next colour and so on. This is the quickest method and something I find quite handy, as it also ensures you always join the colours in the correct order for each and every square.

The Half Granny

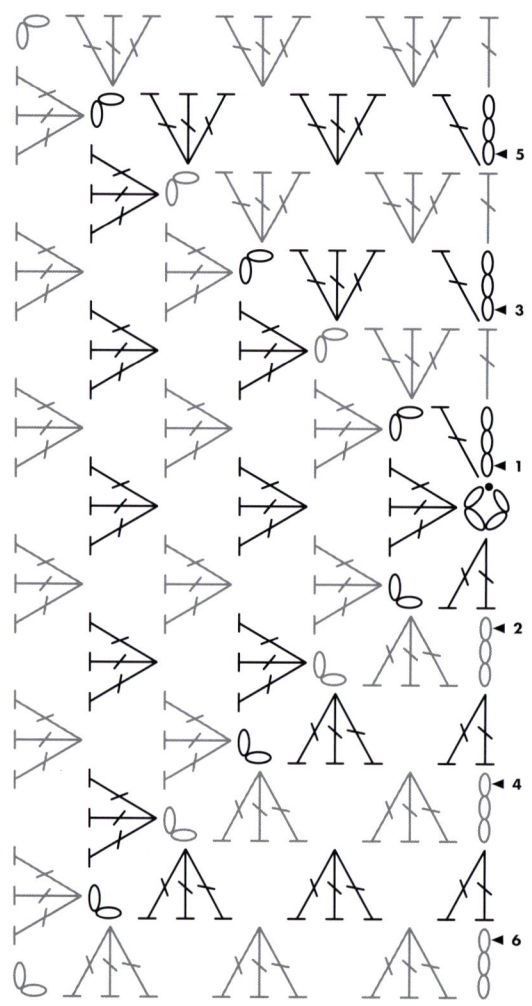

Key

- O ch
- ⊤ tr
- • sl st
- ▶ beginning of round

Projects

- Abstract Squares Tank Top (note that round 5 uses double crochet edging).
- Cozy Cropped Cardigan

These squares are nice to use on the front of a garment so that you can split it in half evenly. They're also good to use instead of a full square when you need to shorten a sleeve.

GRANNY SQUARE TIPS

- Turning your square on every round will prevent 'the granny lean', which can make your square look a little skewed.

- You may only need to lightly block (see page 137) your squares or they might look fine as they are!

The Diagonal and Quarter Granny Square

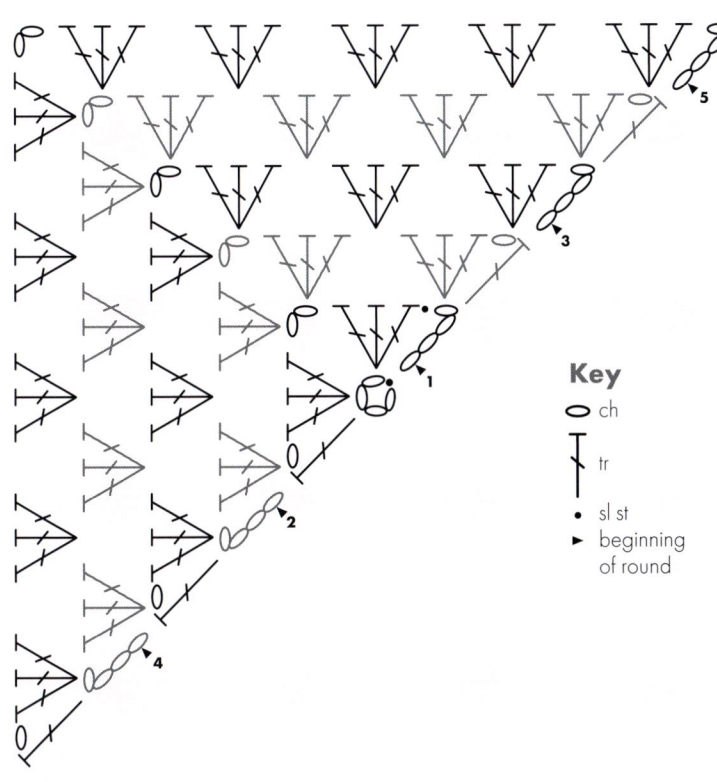

Projects

- Floral Headscarf
- Sixties-Style Mini Dress
- Half & Half Jumper
- Boho-Chic Maxi Waistcoat

Key

○ ch

† tr

• sl st

► beginning of round

These squares are used under the arms of some garments. They provide a nice shape rather than a square-shaped hole.

Projects

Sixties-Style Mini Dress

Quarter granny squares are used in those little gaps where simply nothing else will fit.

Key

○ ch

† tr

• sl st

► beginning of round

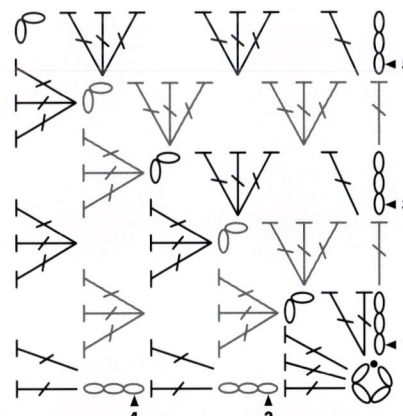

CHAPTER TWO:

The Projects

This chapter contains 15 beautiful, fashion-focused, granny square garments and accessories, including waistcoats, jumpers, hats and bags.

Rainbow Shopper

Classic granny squares are used to create this lovely, fun bag, which is worked in a bright and uplifting rainbow palette.

Tools and materials

Scheepjes Softfun, 60% Cotton, 40% Acrylic, 50g (1¾oz) = 140m (153yd)

Yarn A: Azure 2629 x 2 balls
Yarn B: Pink 2480 x 1 ball
Yarn C: Canary 2518 x 1 ball
Yarn D: Pumpkin 2651 x 1 ball
Yarn E: Hot Pink 2495 x 1 ball
Yarn F: Cool Blue 2603 x 1 ball
Yarn G: Denim 2489 x 1 ball
Size 4.5mm (7) hook
1m (40in) lining fabric
Sewing needle and thread
Yarn needle

Yarn substitutes

Any DK weight yarn would be a suitable substitute.

See also

• The classic granny, page 14

This bag uses a mix of bright colours and pastel tones. Purple acts as the base colour here, but it can easily be swapped out for another colour if you prefer.

Schematic

The numbers above and beside correspond to the colourway of the small squares.

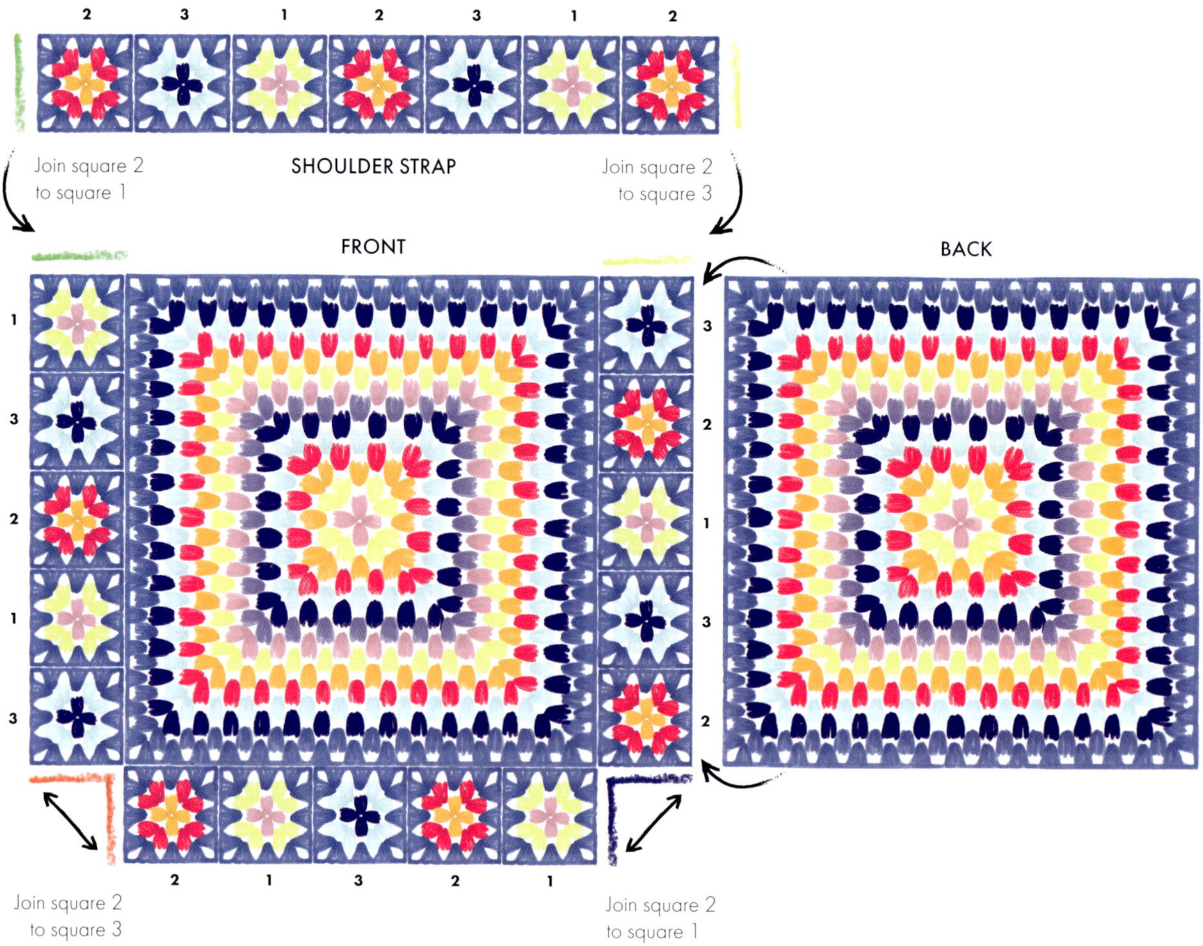

2	3	1	2	3	1	2

SHOULDER STRAP

Join square 2
to square 1

Join square 2
to square 3

FRONT

BACK

1	
3	
2	
1	
3	

3	
2	
1	
3	
2	

2	1	3	2	1

Join square 2
to square 3

Join square 2
to square 1

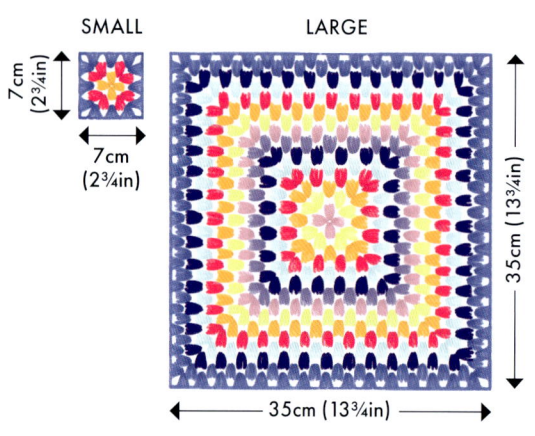

SMALL

LARGE

7cm
(2¾in)

7cm
(2¾in)

35cm (13¾in)

35cm (13¾in)

Tension

- Small granny square measures
  7 x 7cm (2¾ x 2¾in)
- Large granny square measures
  35 x 35cm (13¾ x 13¾in)
- Both made using size 4.5mm (7)
  hook or size required to obtain the
  correct tension.

Large granny square (make two)

Using yarn B, 4 ch, sl st to first ch to form a ring.

Round 1 (RS): 3 ch (counts as first tr here and throughout), 2 tr in ring, 2 ch, [3 tr, 2 ch] three times in ring, sl st to top of beg 3-ch to join, turn. Fasten off.

Round 2 (WS): join yarn C in any corner 2-ch sp, 3 ch, [2 tr, 2 ch, 3 tr] in same 2-ch sp, [3 tr, 2 ch, 3 tr] in each of the next three corner 2-ch sps, sl st to top of beg 3-ch to join, turn.
Fasten off.

Round 3 (RS): join yarn D in any corner 2-ch sp, 3 ch, [2 tr, 2 ch, 3 tr] in same 2-ch sp, 3 tr in space before next 3-tr group, *[3 tr, 2 ch, 3 tr] in corner 2-ch sp, 3 tr in space before next 3-tr group; rep from * twice more, sl st to top of 3-ch to join, turn.
Fasten off.

Round 4 (WS): join yarn E in any corner 2-ch sp, 3 ch, [2 tr, 2 ch, 3 tr] in same 2-ch sp, 3 tr in space between next two 3-tr groups, *[3 tr, 2 ch, 3 tr] in corner 2-ch sp, 3 tr in space before next two 3-tr groups; rep from * twice more, sl st to top of 3-ch to join, turn.

Round 5 (RS): join yarn F in any corner 2-ch sp, 3 ch, [2 tr, 2 ch, 3 tr] in same 2-ch sp, 3 tr in space between each 3-tr group to next corner 2-ch sp, *[3 tr, 2 ch, 3 tr] in corner 2-ch sp, 3 tr in space between each 3-tr group to corner 2-ch sp; rep from * twice more, sl st to top of 3-ch to join, turn.
Fasten off.

Round 6: as round 5 using yarn G.
Round 7: as round 5 using yarn A.
Round 8: as round 5 using yarn B.
Round 9: as round 5 using yarn C.
Round 10: as round 5 using yarn D.
Round 11: as round 5 using yarn E.
Round 12: as round 5 using yarn F.
Round 13: as round 5 using yarn G.
Round 14: as round 5 using yarn A.
Round 15: as round 5 using yarn A.

A lining can add structure and prevent the crochet fabric from getting pulled out of shape. The lining will also prevent your precious items from falling through holes in the textile.

The large granny squares in this book have 15 rounds of vibrant colours, with colours alternating as you complete each round. The square shown here includes seven different colours. You can replicate this combination in your own creations or create your own mix of colours.

Small granny squares (make 22 in total)

These can either be joined by working in blo of each st or by using the continual joining method in round 3. Follow pattern for rounds 1–3 of Large granny square, working the following number of squares in colour combinations as set:

Square 1 (make seven)
Round 1: yarn B.
Round 2: yarn C.
Round 3: yarn A.

Square 2 (make eight)
Round 1: yarn D.
Round 2: yarn E.
Round 3: yarn A.

Square 3 (make seven)
Round 1: yarn G.
Round 2: yarn F.
Round 3: yarn A.

Finishing

1. Join the squares as shown on schematic on page 24. Weave in yarn ends.

2. Place a cardboard base measuring 35 x 6.5cm (13¾ x 2½in) in the bottom of the bag.

3. Take the lining fabric and, using large granny squares and the strap as a guide, cut out two large squares and two long strips of fabric (one for inside the bag and one for the strap) making sure the pieces are slightly larger than your crocheted pieces to allow for a neat, folded edge.

4. Using backstitch (or a sewing machine), sew one fabric strip around three sides of the large lining squares.

5. Hand sew this section of the lining into the fabric bag. Do not sew across the section where the handle meets the bag.

6. Line the handle with the other long fabric strip, hand sewing down each side.

7. Tuck the ends of the strap into the main lining and use a neat whip stitch to close the sections where the strap meets the bag.

Using smaller granny squares for the shoulder strap adds more stability to the bag and will provide more comfort as the wide strap distributes the weight.

Mix & Match Bucket Hat

Bucket hats are a trendy summer accessory, and the perfect way
to add a pop of colour to your wardrobe. Make one for yourself and one for a friend!

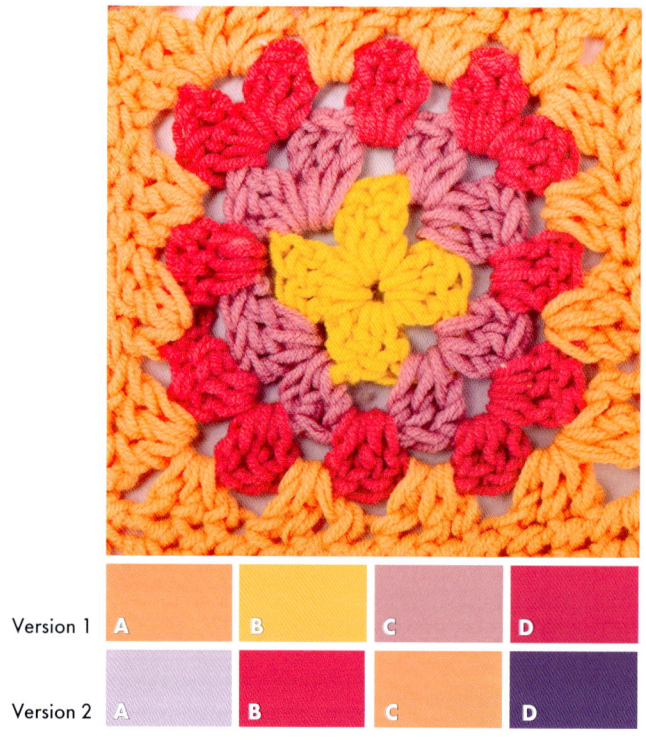

	A	B	C	D
Version 1				
Version 2				

Tools and materials

Scheepjes Softfun, 60% Cotton, 40% Acrylic, 50g (1¾oz) = 140m (153yd)

Version 1
Yarn A: Cantaloupe 2652 x 1 ball
Yarn B: Bumblebee 2518 x 1 ball
Yarn C: Rose 2480 x 1 ball
Yarn D: Hot Pink 2495 x 1 ball

Version 2
Yarn A: Orchid 2657 x 1 ball
Yarn B: Hot Pink 2495 x 1 ball
Yarn C: Soft Coral 2636 x 1 ball
Yarn D: Purple 2463 x 1 ball

Size 4.5mm (7) hook
Yarn needle

Yarn substitutes

Any DK weight yarn would be a suitable substitute.

See also
• The classic granny, page 14

This piece is quick to work up and is shown in two colourways: one with purple as a base colour and one with orange.

Schematic

You need just five granny squares for this project.

Join squares

Use the main colour of your granny square to create the crown and the brim (see pages 28–29).

56cm (22in)

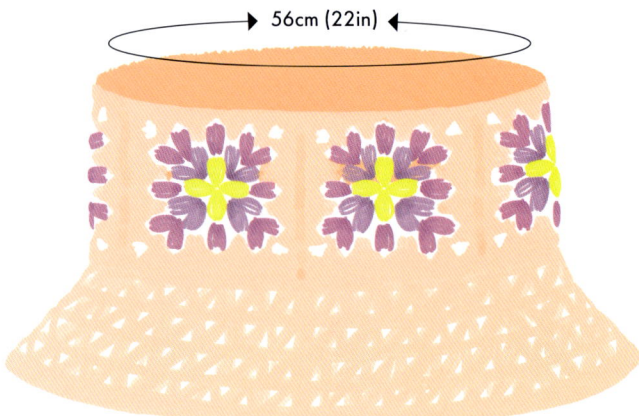

You can replicate this fun bucket hat with your own colour choices.

11cm (4¼in)

11cm (4¼in)

Tension

- Granny square measures 11 x 11cm (4¼ x 4¼in)
- Made using a size 4.5mm (7) hook or hook size required to obtain the correct tension.

Special stitches

(hat brim – see page 33)

Reverse double crochet (rdc): working from left to right, insert hook in next stitch, yo and pull up a loop; yo, and draw through both loops on hook.

Increases in rounds 1, 2 and 4 mean the brim gradually increases in size as you work it. The resulting flexible brim can be gently positioned with your hands into your preferred shape.

Granny square (make five)

Using yarn B, 4 ch, sl st to first ch to form a ring.

Round 1 (RS): 3 ch (counts as 1 tr here and throughout) 2 tr in ring, 2 ch, [3 tr, 2 ch] three times in ring, join with sl st to top of 3-ch, turn. Fasten off yarn B. Join yarn C in any corner 2-ch sp.

Round 2 (WS): 3 ch, [2 tr, 2 ch, 3 tr] in same 2-ch sp, [3 tr, 2 ch, 3 tr] in each 2-ch sp around, sl st to join, turn.

Fasten off yarn C. Join yarn D in any corner 2-ch sp.

Round 3 (RS): 3 ch, [2 tr, 2 ch, 3 tr] in same 2-ch sp, 3 tr in sp between 3-tr groups, *[3 tr, 2 ch, 3 tr] in next 2-ch sp, 3 tr in next sp; rep from * twice more, sl st to top of 3-ch, turn.

Fasten off yarn D. Join yarn A in any corner 2-ch sp.

Round 4 (WS): 3 ch, [2 tr, 2 ch, 3 tr] in same 2-ch sp, 3 tr in sp between next two 3-tr groups, *[3 tr, 2 ch, 3 tr] in next 2-ch sp, 3 tr in sp between next two 3-tr groups; rep from * twice more, sl st to top of 3-ch.

Fasten off.

Join squares

Using yarn A, sew all five squares together with a neat whip stitch to make a band.

Top edge

Rejoin yarn A in any corner ch sp of any square with 1 ch (does not count as a st).

Round 1: 1 dc in each st and in each corner ch sp of each square around, sl st to join (70 sts).

Round 2: 1 ch (does not count as a st), [dc2tog, 12 dc] four times, dc2tog, 10 dc, dc2tog, sl st to join (64 sts).

Fasten off.

Crown

Using yarn A, 4 ch, sl st to join to a ring.

Round 1: 2 ch (counts as 1 htr), 7 htr in ring, sl st to beg 2-ch to join (8 sts).

Round 2: 2 ch, 1 htr in same st, 2 htr in each of next 7 sts, sl st to join (16 sts).

Round 3: 2 ch, 1 htr in same st, 1 htr, [2 htr in next st, 1 htr] around, sl st to join (24 sts).

Round 4: 2 ch, 1 htr in same st, 2 htr, [2 htr in next st, 2 htr] around, sl st to join (32 sts).

Round 5: 2 ch, 1 htr in same st, 3 htr, [2 htr in next st, 3 htr] around, sl st to join (40 sts).

Round 6: 2 ch, 1 htr in same st, 4 htr, [2 htr in next st, 4 htr] around, sl st to join (48 sts).

Round 7: 2 ch, 1 htr in same st, 5 htr, [2 htr in next st, 5 htr] around, sl st to join (56 sts).

Round 8: 2 ch, 1 htr in same st, 6 htr, [2 htr in next st, 6 htr] around, sl st to join (64 sts).

Fasten off leaving a long tail. Use the tail to sew the crown to the top of the hat band with a neat whip stitch matching stitch for stitch.

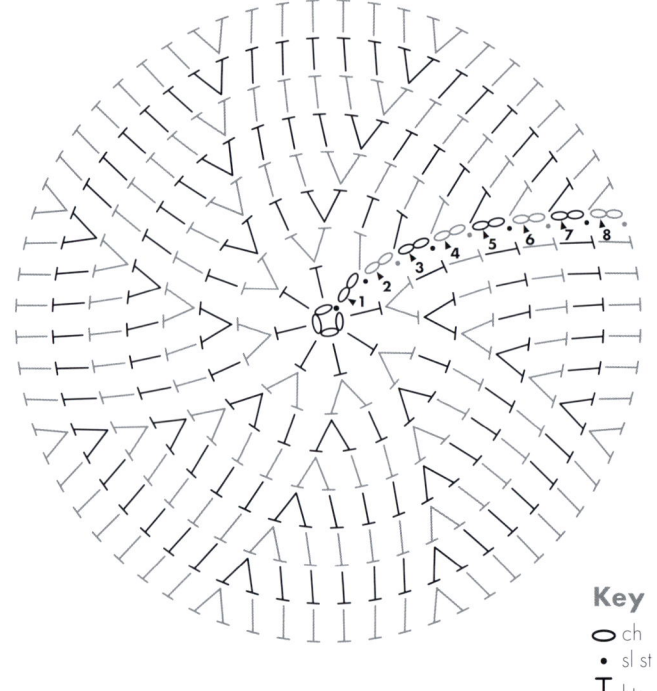

Key

⬭ ch

• sl st

⊤ htr

▶ beginning of round

If you want to make a larger hat, use a larger hook for the crown – try going up by half a hook size.

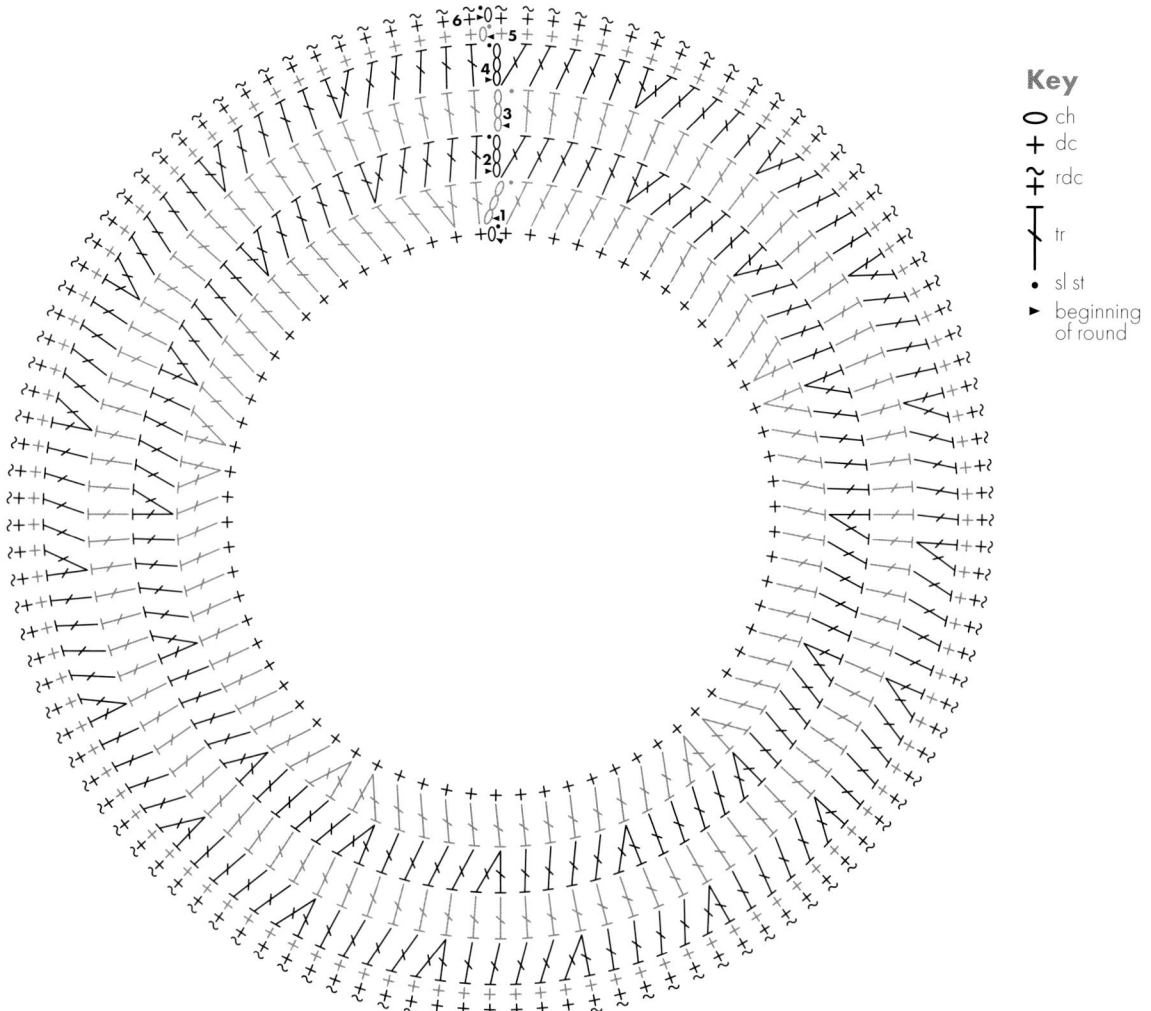

Key

○ ch

+ dc

⁺̃ rdc

‖ tr

• sl st

▶ beginning
of round

Brim

With the bottom edge of the hat facing, rejoin yarn A in any corner ch sp of any square with 1 ch (does not count as a st).

Foundation round: 1 dc in each st and in each corner ch sp of each square around, sl st to join (70 sts).

Round 1: 3 ch (counts as 1 tr), 1 tr in same st, 2 tr in next st, 12 tr, [2 tr in each of next 2 sts, 12 tr], sl st to join, turn (80 sts).

Round 2: 3 ch, 1 tr in same st, 4 tr, [2 tr in next st, 4 tr] around, sl st to join, turn (96 sts).

Round 3: 3 ch, 1 tr in each tr around, sl st to join, turn.

Round 4: 3 ch, 1 tr in same st, 4 tr, [2 tr in next st, 4 tr] to last st, 1 tr, sl st to join, turn (115 sts).

Round 5: 1 ch, 1 dc in each st around, sl st to join.

Round 6: 1 ch, 1 rdc (see Special stitches) in each st around. Fasten off.

Finishing

Weave in yarn ends.

Floral Headscarf

This quick make bandanna is ideal for lazy beach days basking in the sun. Or maybe wear it with your favourite sundress for a summer garden party!

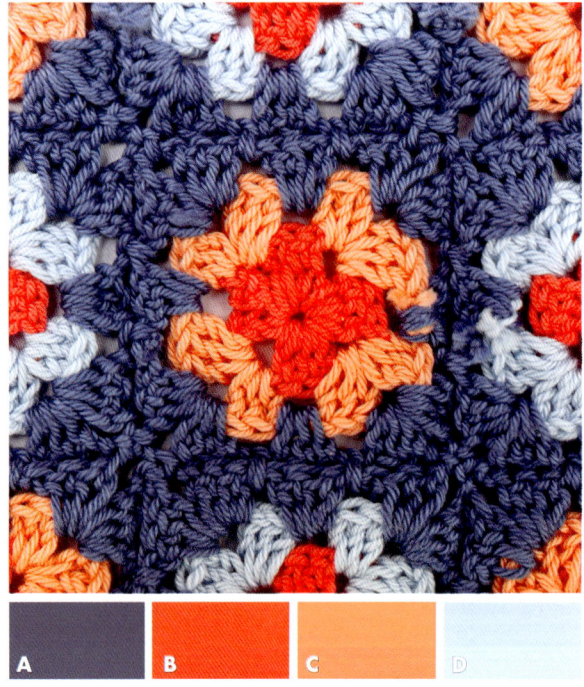

| A | B | C | D |

Tools and materials

Scheepjes Catona 100% cotton
50g (1¾oz) = 125m (27¼yd)
Yarn A: Bluebird 247 x 1 ball
Scheepjes Catona 100% cotton
25g (⅞oz) = 62.5m (68¼yd)
Yarn B: Cornelia Rose 256 x 1 ball
Yarn C: Light Coral 264 x 1 ball
Yarn D: Bluebell 173 x 1 ball

Size 3.5mm (E/4) hook
Yarn needle

Yarn substitutes

Any 4-ply/fingering weight cotton
yarn would be a suitable substitute.

See also

• The classic granny, page 14
• Diagonal half granny, page 19

Although this stylish headscarf is designed to keep your hair away from your face, it also looks chic when styled with face-framing strands escaping from the front.

Schematic

The numbers above the squares correspond to the colourway of that square.

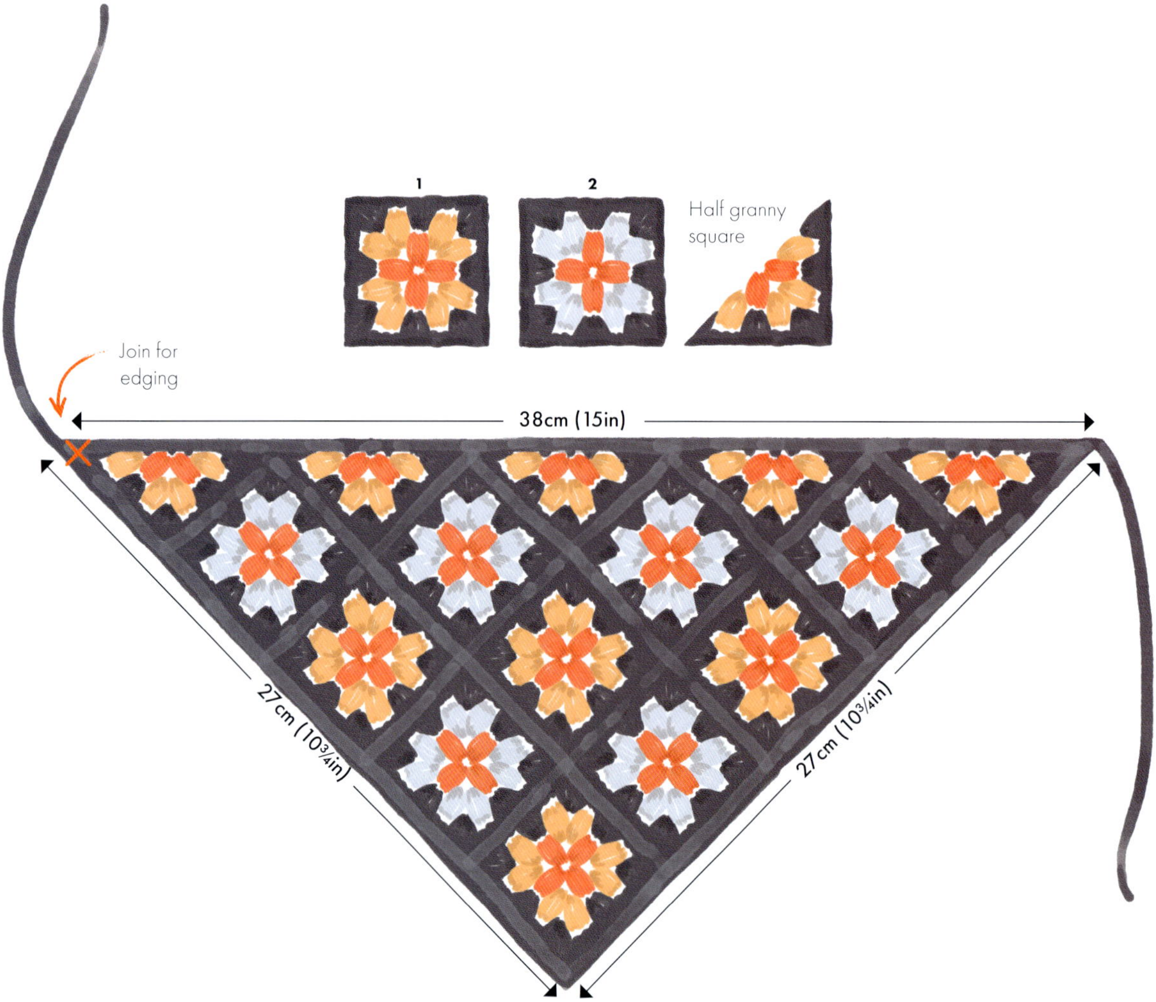

1 **2** Half granny square

Join for edging

38cm (15in)

27cm (10¾in)

27cm (10¾in)

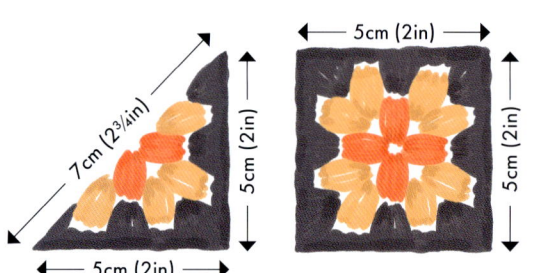

5cm (2in)

5cm (2in)

7cm (2¾in)

5cm (2in)

5cm (2in)

Tension

- Full granny square measures 5 x 5cm (2 x 2in).
- Half diagonal granny square measures 5 x 5 x 7cm (2 x 2 x 2¾in).
- Made using size 3.5mm (E/4) hook or size required to obtain correct tension.

Granny square (make ten in total)

Square 1 (make four)
Round 1: yarn B.
Round 2: yarn C.
Round 3: yarn A.

Square 2 (make six)
Round 1: yarn B.
Round 2: yarn D.
Round 3: yarn A.

Using yarn B, 4 ch, sl st to first ch to form a ring.
Round 1 (RS): 3 ch (counts as 1 tr here and throughout) 2 tr in ring, 2 ch, [3 tr, 2 ch] three times in ring, join with sl st to top of 3-ch, turn. Fasten off yarn B, join yarn C (D) in any corner ch sp.
Round 2 (WS): 3 ch, [2 tr, 2 ch, 3 tr] in same 2-ch sp, [3 tr, 2 ch, 3 tr] in each 2-ch sp around, sl st to

join, turn.
Fasten off yarn C (D), join yarn A in any corner 2-ch sp.
Round 3 (RS): 3 ch, [2 tr, 2 ch, 3 tr] in same 2-ch sp, 3 tr in sp between 3-tr groups, *[3 tr, 2 ch, 3 tr] in next 2-ch sp, 3 tr in next sp; rep from * twice more, sl st to top of 3-ch.
Fasten off.

If you have long hair, the tie will not be visible. However, you can increase the number of chains if you prefer a longer, more visbile tie.

The headscarf is a versatile accessory. It can protect your head from the sun or it could be worn round the neck as a neckerchief.

Half diagonal granny square

(make five)

Using yarn B, 4 ch, sl st to first ch to form a ring.

Round 1 (RS): 4 ch (counts as first tr + 1 ch), [3 tr, 2 ch, 3 tr] in ring, 1 ch, 1 tr in ring, turn.

Fasten off yarn B. Join yarn C into top of last tr of round 1.

Round 2 (WS): 4 ch, 3 tr in 1-ch sp, [3 tr, 2 ch, 3 tr] in corner 2-ch sp, 3 tr in 1-ch sp, 1 ch, 1 tr in third of 4-ch, turn.

Fasten off yarn C. Join yarn A in top of last tr of round 2.

Round 3: 4 ch, 3 tr in 1-ch sp, 3 tr in space before next 3-tr group, [3 tr, 2 ch, 3 tr] in corner 2-ch sp, 3 tr in space before next 3-tr group, 3 tr in 1-ch sp, 1 ch, 1 tr in third of 4-ch.

Fasten off yarn A.

Joining

Join squares together using the schematic as a guide. Join using whip stitch through the back loops on WS or using the continual joining method (see page 136).

Edging

Using yarn A, work 40 ch (for first tie), now with RS facing, starting in corner marked with red 'X' on schematic, cont as foll:

Round 1: 1 dc in each st and ch sp to corner, 2 dc in corner ch sp, 1 dc in each st and ch sp to next corner, 41 ch, 1 dc in bottom bump of second ch from hook and in each of next 39 ch (for second tie), work 1 dc in centre of each square and 2 dc under each row end along long edge, now work 1 dc in bottom bump of each of beg 40 ch, turn.

Round 2: 1 ch, 1 dc in each st along first tie, along long edge and along second tie.

Fasten off.

Finishing

Weave in all ends and lightly block.

Beach Day Headband

This quick make, worked in bright, sunny colours is perfect for a day at the beach or to complete your festival outfit. Tie it in a bow or simply tie and hang loose.

Tools and materials

Scheepjes Cotton 8 4ply,
100% Cotton, 50g (1¾oz) =
170m (186yd)
Yarn A: Ochre 722 x 1 ball
Yarn B: Orange Pink 650 x 1 ball
Yarn C: Fuchsia 720 x 1 ball
Yarn D: Orange 716 x 1 ball
Yarn E: Violet 529 x 1 ball

Size 3mm (C/2 or D/3) hook
Yarn needle

Yarn substitutes

Any 4-ply weight yarn would be a
suitable substitute.

See also

• The classic granny square, page 14

This headband is constructed from four four-round granny squares, which produces a band wide enough to hold back long hair.

Schematic

The numbers below the squares correspond to the colourway of that square.

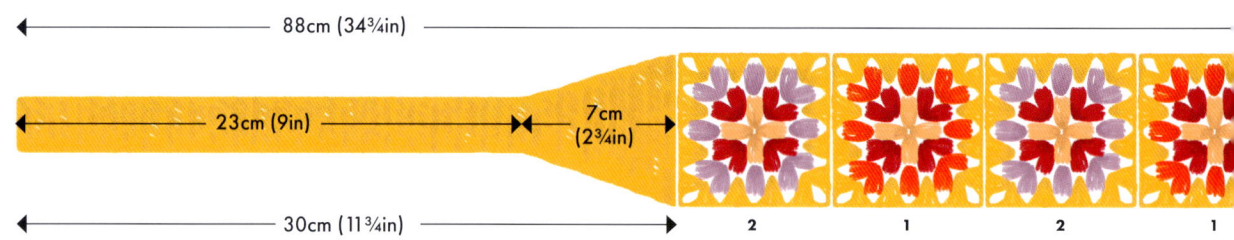

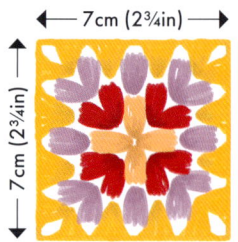

Tension

- Granny square measures 7 x 7cm (2¾ x 2¾in) square.
- Made using size 3mm (C/2 or D/3) hook or size required to obtain the correct tension.

Granny square (make four in total)

Square 1 (make two)
Round 1: yarn B.
Round 2: yarn C.
Round 3: yarn D.
Round 4: yarn A.

Square 2 (make two)
Round 1: yarn B.
Round 2: yarn C.
Round 3: yarn E.
Round 4: yarn A.

Using the suggested yarn for your choice of square, 4 ch, sl st to first ch to form a ring.
Round 1 (RS): 3 ch (counts as first tr here and throughout), 2 tr in ring, 2 ch, [3 tr, 2 ch] three times in ring,

sl st to top of beg 3-ch to join, turn. Fasten off.
Round 2 (WS): join next yarn shade in any corner 2-ch sp, 3 ch, [2 tr, 2 ch, 3 tr] in same 2-ch sp, [3 tr, 2 ch, 3 tr] in each of the next three corner 2-ch sps, sl st to top of beg 3-ch to join, turn. Fasten off.
Round 3 (RS): join next yarn shade in any corner 2-ch sp, 3 ch, [2 tr, 2 ch, 3 tr] in same 2-ch sp, 3 tr in space before next 3-tr group, *[3 tr, 2 ch, 3 tr] in corner 2-ch sp, 3 tr in space before next 3-tr group; rep from * twice more, sl st to top of 3-ch to join, turn.
Round 4 (WS): join yarn A in any

corner 2-ch sp, 3 ch, [2 tr, 2 ch, 3 tr] in same 2-ch sp, 3 tr in space between next two 3-tr groups, *[3 tr, 2 ch, 3 tr] in corner 2-ch sp, 3 tr in space before next two 3-tr groups; rep from * twice more, sl st to top of 3-ch to join, turn.

Join squares together into a strip of four using the continual joining method or stitch together with a neat whip stitch.

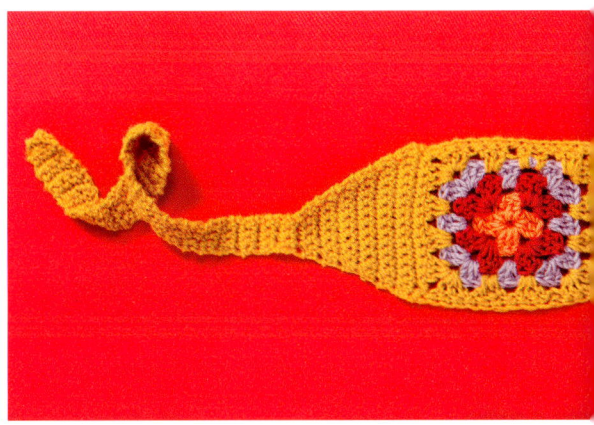

1.5cm (½in)

Before fastening off, try the headband on and see if you would like to add more rows to the ties according to your preference.

Long side edging

Join yarn A in top corner of one long side with 1 ch, work 1 row in dc along long edge distributing 14 sts per square and ending in corner ch sp of last square.

Fasten off.
Repeat on second long edge.

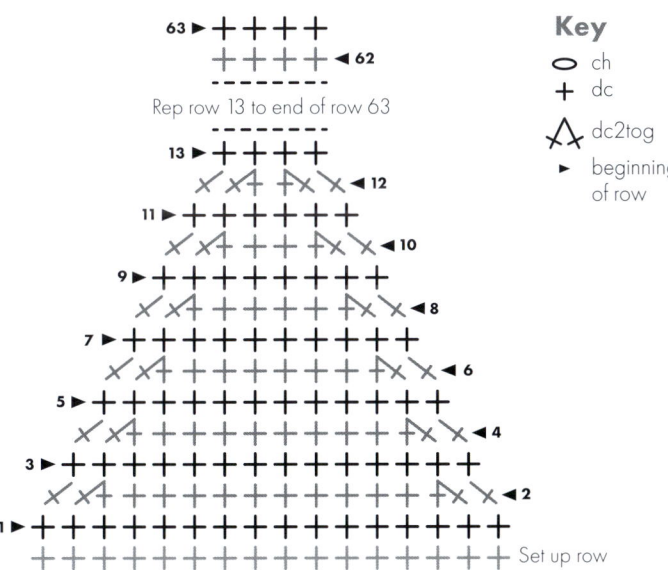

63 ▶ + + + +
+ + + + ◀ 62
- - - - - - - -
Rep row 13 to end of row 63
- - - - - - - -
13 ▶ + + + +
✕ ✕ ⋏ + ✕ ✕ ◀ 12
11 ▶ + + + + + +
✕ ✕ + + + + ✕ ✕ ◀ 10
9 ▶ + + + + + + + +
✕ ✕ + + + + + ✕ ✕ ◀ 8
7 ▶ + + + + + + + + + +
✕ ✕ + + + + + + ✕ ✕ ◀ 6
5 ▶ + + + + + + + + + + + +
✕ ✕ + + + + + + + ✕ ✕ ◀ 4
3 ▶ + + + + + + + + + + + + + +
✕ ✕ + + + + + + + + ✕ ✕ ◀ 2
1 ▶ + + + + + + + + + + + + + + + +
+ + + + + + + + + + + + + + + + Set up row

Key
○ ch
+ dc
⋏ dc2tog
▶ beginning of row

Short edges and ties

Join yarn A under first dc worked on long side edging row, work 1 dc under this row end, then work 14 dc along short end of square and 1 dc under bottom long side edging row, turn (16 dc).
Row 1: 1 dc in each dc to end, turn.
Row 2: 1 dc, dc2tog, dc to last 3 dc, dc2tog, 1 dc, turn (14 dc).
Rows 3–12: rep rows 1 and 2 (4 dc).
Rows 13–62: 1 dc in each dc to end, turn.
Row 63: 1 dc in each dc to end.
Fasten off.
Repeat on second short end.

Finishing

Weave in all yarn ends and lightly block.

Abstract Squares Tank Top

These small granny motifs pay homage to the artist Kandinsky and his famous squares painting. Wear it alone or pop it on over your favourite shirt.

Tools and materials

Scheepjes Cotton 8 4ply, 100% Cotton, 50g (1¾oz) = 170m (186yd)

Yarn A: Natural 501 x 6(7:8:9:10:11:12:14) balls

Yarn B: Pink 719 x 1(1:1:1:1:1:1:1) ball

Yarn C: Orange 716 x 2(2:2:2:3:3:3:3) balls

Yarn D: Light Orange 639 x 2(2:2:2:3:3:3:3) balls

Yarn E: Ochre 722 x 1(1:1:1:1:1:1:1) ball

Yarn F: Turquoise 712 x 2(2:2:2:3:3:3:3) balls

Yarn G: Light Turquoise 622 x 2(2:2:2:3:3:3:3) balls

Size 3.5mm (E/4) hook

Size 5mm (H/8) hook

Yarn needles

Yarn substitutes

Any 4-ply weight yarn would be a suitable substitute.

See also

• The classic granny, page 14
• The half granny, page 18

This tank top will make any shirt a lot more interesting. Choose your granny square colour scheme to suit your wardrobe.

Sizes

To fit	1	2	3	4	5	6	7	8	
Actual chest approx.	85	93	101	113	124	133	145	152	cm
	33½	36½	39¾	44½	48¾	52	57	60	in
Length approx.	53	53	57	57	53.5	58	58	63	cm
	21	21	22½	22½	21	22¾	22¾	24¾	in

LARGE
(To end of round 5)

4.75cm
(1¾in)

9.5cm (3½in)

8.5cm (3in)

4.25cm
(1½in)

MEDIUM
(To end of round 4)

LARGE (To end of round 5)

9.5cm (3½in)

9.5cm (3½in)

MEDIUM
(To end of round 4)

8.5cm (3in)

8.5cm (3in)

Tension

- Full medium squares measure 8.5 x 8.5cm (3 x 3in) and full large squares measure 9.5 x 9.5cm (3½ x 3½in).
- Half medium squares measure 8.5 x 4.25cm (3 x 1½in) and half large squares measure. 9.5 x 4.75cm (3½ x 1¾in).
- Made using size 3.5mm (E/4) hook or size required to obtain the correct tension.

Schematic

Pink cross indicates joining point for widening rows

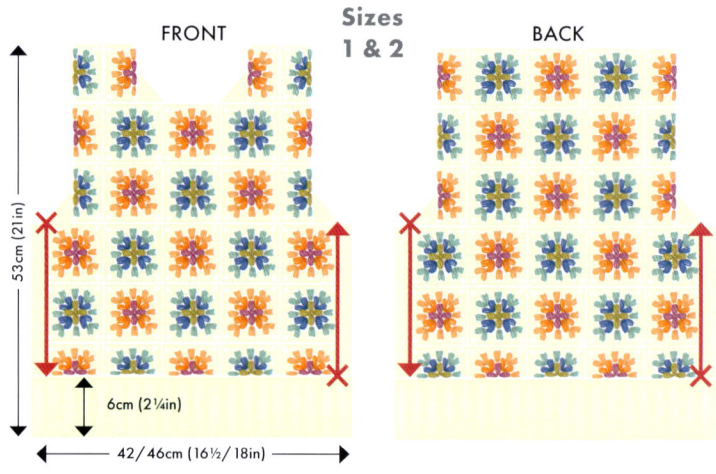

Sizes 1 & 2

FRONT   BACK

53cm (21in)

6cm (2¼in)

42/46cm (16½/18in)

Using medium squares
Work two widening rows on Size 2 only

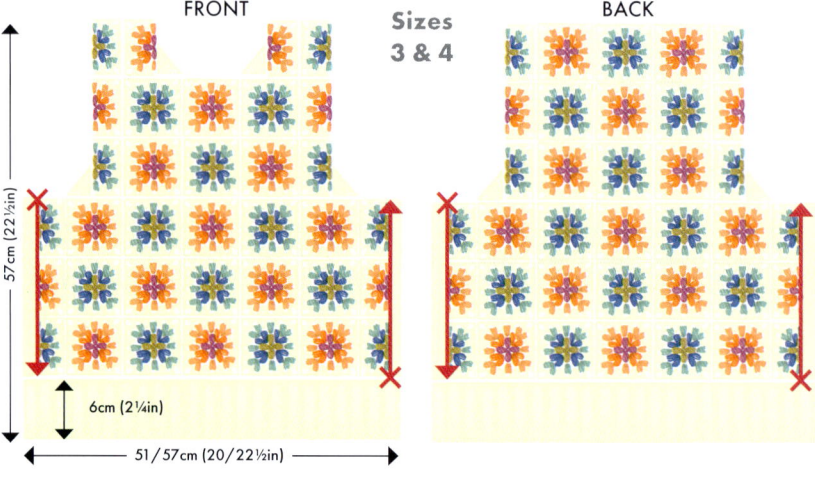

Sizes 3 & 4

FRONT   BACK

57cm (22½in)

6cm (2¼in)

51/57cm (20/22½in)

Using medium squares
Work three widening rows each side on Size 4 only

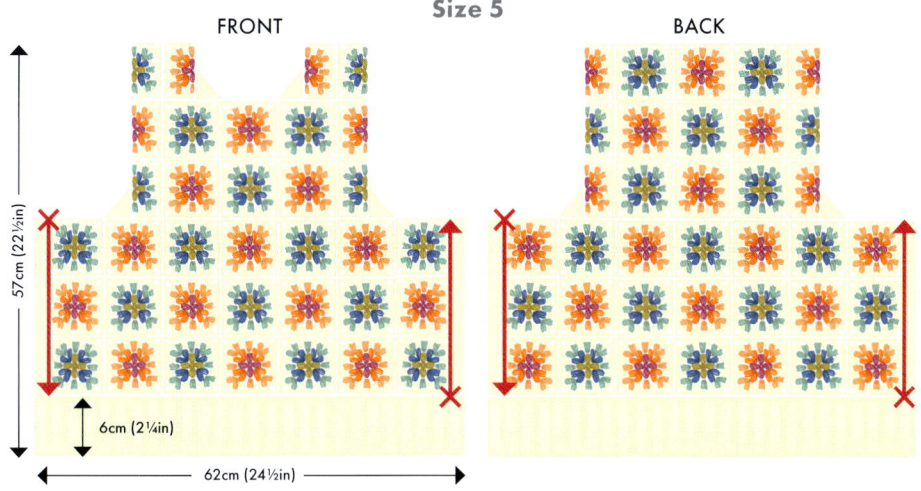

Size 5

FRONT

BACK

57cm (22½in)

62cm (24½in)

6cm (2¼in)

Using large squares
And one row each side for widening

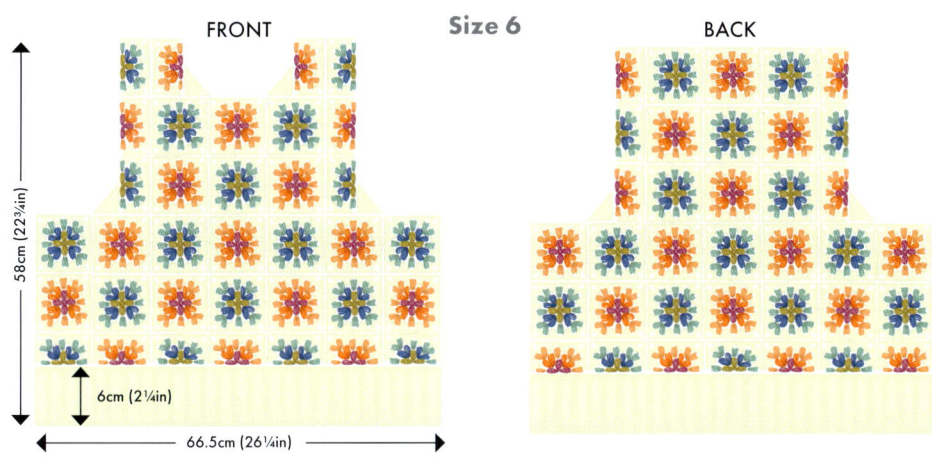

Size 6

FRONT

BACK

58cm (22¾in)

66.5cm (26¼in)

6cm (2¼in)

Using large squares

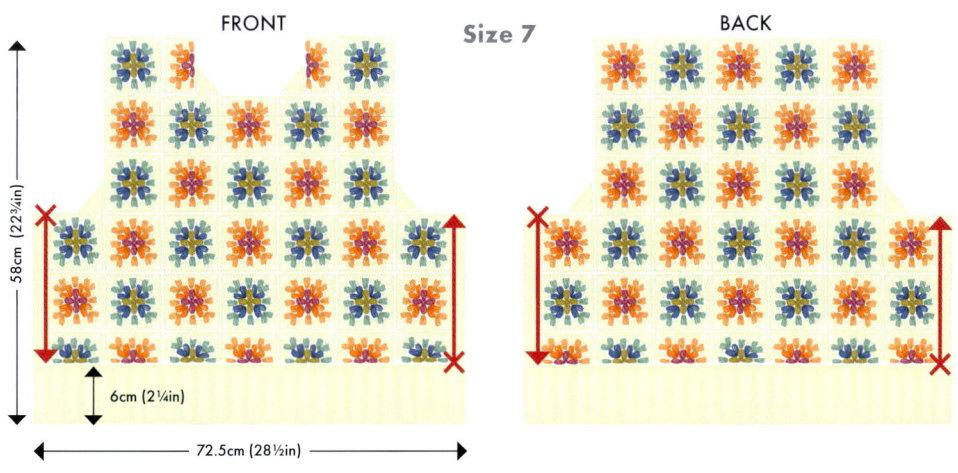

Size 7

FRONT

BACK

58cm (22¾in)

72.5cm (28½in)

6cm (2¼in)

Using large squares
Work three widening rows each side

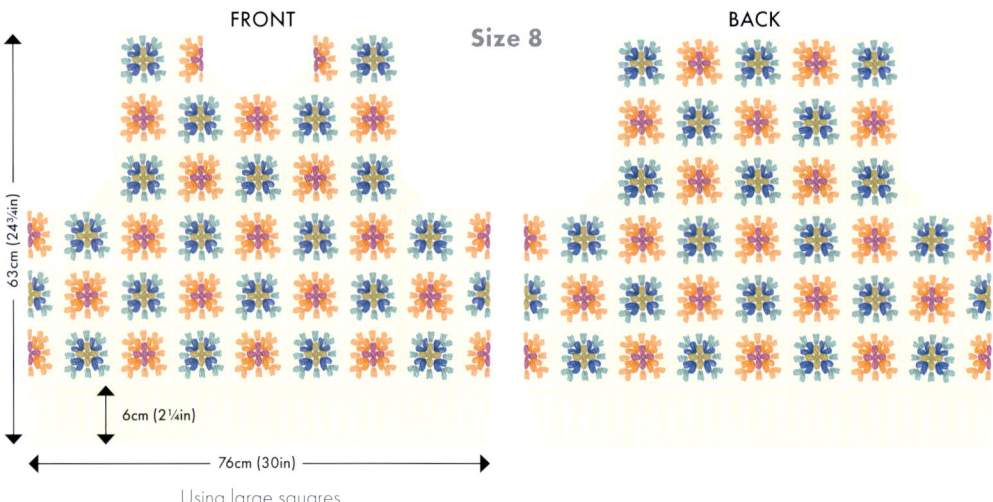

FRONT   Size 8   BACK

63cm (24¾in)

6cm (2¼in)

76cm (30in)

Using large squares

Pattern notes

Sizes 1–5
Make all full and half squares in medium 8.5cm (3in) size (to the end of round 4).

Sizes 6–8
Make all full and half squares in large 9.5cm (3½in) size (to the end of round 5).

The squares used in the tank top are organized into two different colourways:

Square 1

Square 2

Half square 1

Half square 2

Square 1
Round 1: yarn B.
Round 2: yarn C.
Round 3: yarn D.
Rounds 4 and 5: yarn A.

Square 2
Round 1: yarn E.
Round 2: yarn F.
Round 3: yarn G.
Rounds 4 and 5: yarn A.

Make the following number of squares and corners in the two different colourways. Use the schematic on the previous spread to determine the size of the square (medium or large):

Size	1	2	3	4	5	6	7	8
Full squares: Square 1	17	17	22	24	28	21	27	32
Full squares: Square 2	18	18	20	22	29	22	28	37
Half squares: Square 1	13	13	12	10	8	15	9	10
Half squares: Square 2	11	11	16	16	6	13	7	4
Corner	6	6	6	6	6	6	6	6

Full square

Using a size 3.5mm (E/4) hook and suggested yarn, 4 ch, sl st to first ch to form a ring.

Round 1 (RS): 3 ch (counts as first tr here and throughout), 2 tr in ring, 2 ch, [3 tr, 2 ch] three times in ring, sl st to top of beg 3-ch to join, turn. Fasten off.

Round 2 (WS): join next yarn shade in any corner 2-ch sp, 3 ch, [2 tr, 2 ch, 3 tr] in same 2-ch sp, [3 tr, 2 ch, 3 tr] in each of the next three corner 2-ch sps, sl st to top of beg 3-ch to join, turn. Fasten off.

Round 3 (RS): join next yarn shade in any corner 2-ch sp, 3 ch, [2 tr, 2 ch, 3 tr] in same 2-ch sp, 3 tr in space before next 3-tr group, *[3 tr, 2 ch, 3 tr] in corner 2-ch sp, 3 tr in space before next 3-tr group; rep from * twice more, sl st to top of 3-ch to join, turn.

Round 4 (WS): join yarn A in any corner 2-ch sp, 3 ch, [2 tr, 2 ch, 3 tr] in same 2-ch sp, 3 tr in space between next two 3-tr groups, *[3 tr, 2 ch, 3 tr] in corner 2-ch sp, 3 tr in space before next two 3-tr groups; rep from * twice more, sl st to top of 3-ch to join, turn.

Sizes 1–5

Fasten off.

Sizes 6, 7 and 8 only

Round 5 (RS): work 1 dc in each tr and [1 dc, 2 ch, 1 dc] in each corner 2-ch sp around, sl st to first sc to join.
Fasten off.

Half square

Using a size 3.5mm (E/4) hook and suggested yarn, 4 ch, sl st to first ch to form a ring.

Round 1 (RS): 3 ch (counts as first tr here and throughout) 1 tr, 2 ch, 3 tr, 2 ch, 2 tr in ring, turn. Fasten off.

Round 2 (WS): join next yarn shade in top of last tr, 3 ch, [3 tr, 2 ch, 3 tr] in each of next two 2-ch sps, 1 tr in last tr, turn. Fasten off.

Round 3 (RS): join next yarn shade in top of last tr, 3 ch, 1 tr in space between first tr and next 3 tr, [3 tr, 2 ch, 3 tr] in corner 2-ch sp, 3 tr in space between next 3 tr, [3 tr, 2 ch, 3 tr] in next corner 2-ch sp, 1 tr in space between 3 tr and last tr, 1 tr in last tr, turn.

Fasten off.

Round 4 (WS): join yarn A in top of last tr, 3 ch, 3 tr in space before first 3 tr, [3 tr, 2 ch, 3 tr] in corner 2-ch sp, 3 tr in space between next two sets of 3 tr, [3 tr, 2 ch, 3 tr] in corner 2-ch sp, 3 tr in space before last 2 tr, 1 tr in last tr, turn.

Sizes 1–5

Fasten off.

Sizes 6, 7 and 8 only

Round 5 (RS): work 1 dc in each tr and [1 dc, 2 ch, 1 dc] in each corner 2-ch sp around three sides only. Fasten off.

The ribbed neckline and armholes provide a neat and fitted edge finish to the tank top.

CORNER

Key

○ ch

† tr

• sl st

► beginning of round

The ribbed welt is created by working into the back loops of the previous row.

Corner

Make six using yarn A only.
Using a size 5mm (H/8) hook and yarn A, 4 ch, sl st to first ch to form a ring.
Row 1 (RS): 3 ch, 3 tr, 2 ch, 4 tr in ring.
Fasten off.

Joining

Using a neat whip stitch, join the squares as shown on the schematic to create the front and back sections.

Widening rows

Sizes 2, 4, 5 and 7 only
Row 1: with RS facing rejoin yarn A at point marked with pink cross (as shown on schematic), work 3 ch (counts as first tr), now work 1 tr in each st and ch sp to bottom edge, turn.

Size 5
Fasten off.

Sizes 2, 4 and 7 only
Row 2: 3 ch, tr to end, turn.
Size 2: fasten off.

Sizes 4 and 7 only
Row 3: 3ch, tr to end, turn.
Fasten off.
Repeat along each side as indicated on the schematic.

Assembly

Using whip stitch, join the front to the back at the shoulder seams and join the side seams.

Ribbed welt

Rejoin yarn A to bottom edge inside seam.
Set-up round: work 1 dc around entire bottom edge of garment working 1 dc under each dc widening row end, 2 dc under each tr row end, and 1 dc in each st and ch sp around, sl st to top of first dc and work 14 ch.
Row 1: 1 dc in second ch from hook and in each of next 12 ch, sl st in next tr of set-up round, sl st in foll dc, turn (13 tr).
Row 2: 13 dc blo to end, 1 ch, turn.
Row 3: 13 dc blo to end, sl st in next st of set-up round, sl st in foll st, turn.
Row 4: 13 dc blo to end, 1 ch, turn.
Rep rows 3 and 4 around entire bottom edge of garment until all dc sts of set-up round are used up.
Fasten off leaving a long tail. Use tail to join ends of welt using a neat whip stitch.

Armbands

Set-up round: with RS facing, join yarn A at top of seam at underarm, 1 ch, work in dc around armhole opening working 1 dc in each st and ch sp around, 6 ch.

Row 1: 1 dc in second ch from hook and in each of next 4 ch, sl st in next st of set-up round, sl st in foll dc, turn (5 dc).

Row 2: 5 dc blo to end, 1 ch, turn.

Row 3: 5 dc blo to end, sl st in next st of set-up round, sl st in foll st, turn.

Row 4: 5 dc blo to end, 1 ch, turn.

Rep rows 3 and 4 around armhole until all dc sts of set-up round are used up.

Fasten off leaving a long tail.

Use tail to join ends of armbands using a neat whip stitch.

Neck edging

With RS facing rejoin yarn A at centre back of neck edge.

Work as for armbands.

Finishing

Weave in all yarn ends and lightly block.

For a warmer tank top, use a woollen yarn that crochets to the same tension, rather than cotton.

Bright & Breezy Tote Bag

Granny squares are used to create this lovely, fun bag, worked in a bright and breezy, uplifting colour palette.

Tools and materials

Scheepjes Catona 100% Cotton, 50g (1¾oz) = 125m (27¼yd)

Yarn A: Jet Black 110 x 3 balls

Yarn B: Rich Coral 410 x 1 ball

Yarn C: Sweet Orange 411 x 1 ball

Yarn D: Apple Granny 513 x 1 ball

Yarn E: Tulip 222 x 1 ball

Yarn F: Vivid Blue 146 x 1 ball

Yarn G: Cyan 397 x 1 ball

Yarn H: Shocking Pink 114 x 1 ball

Yarn I: Lavender 520 x 1 ball

Size 3.5mm (E/4) hook

Yarn needle

2 x 15cm (6in) diameter bamboo ring bag handles

Yarn substitutes

Any DK weight yarn that works to the same tension would be a suitable substitute.

See also

• The classic granny square, page 14

The bamboo handle instantly gives this bag a boho, summer vibe; perfect for shopping, an evening out or for your summer holiday.

Schematic

The numbers next to the squares correspond to the colourway of that square (see page 56).

FRONT

Please note the top section of the back is made by working along the top row of the granny squares.

BACK

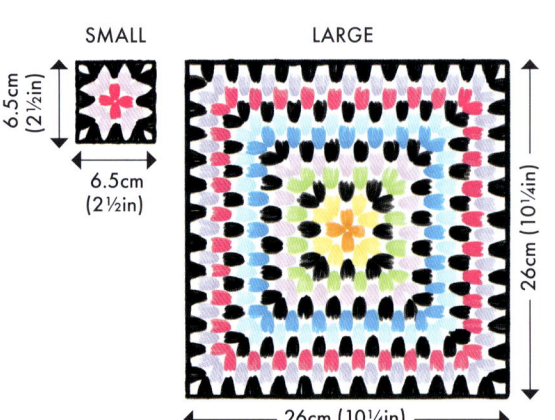

SMALL

6.5cm (2½in)

6.5cm (2½in)

LARGE

26cm (10¼in)

26cm (10¼in)

Tension

- Small granny square measures 6.5 x 6.5cm (2½ x 2½in) using size 3.5mm (E/4) hook.
- Large granny square measures 26 x 26cm (10¼ x 10¼in) using size 3.5mm (E/4) hook.

Large granny square (make two)

With yarn B, 4 ch, sl st to first ch to form ring.

Round 1 (RS): 3 ch (counts as 1 tr here and throughout) 2 tr in ring, 2 ch, (3 tr, 2 ch) three times in ring, join with sl st to top of 3-ch, turn. Change to yarn C.

Round 2 (WS): 3 ch, (2 tr, 2 ch, 3 tr) in same 2-ch sp, (3 tr, 2 ch, 3 tr) in each 2-ch sp, sl st to join, turn. Change to yarn A.

Round 3: 3 ch, 2 tr in sp between 3-tr groups, (3 tr, 2 ch, 3 tr) in next 2-ch sp, *3 tr in next sp, (3 tr, 2 ch, 3 tr) in next 2-ch sp; rep from * twice more, sl st to top of 3-ch, turn. Change to yarn D.

Round 4: 3 ch, 2 tr in sp between 3-tr groups, (3 tr, 2 ch, 3 tr) in next 2-ch sp, *3 tr in each sp to next corner 2-ch sp, (3 tr, 2 ch, 3 tr) in 2-ch sp; rep from * twice more, 3 tr in next sp, sl st to top of 3-ch, turn.

Change to yarn E.

Round 5: 3 ch, 2 tr in same sp, (3 tr, 2 ch, 3 tr) in next ch-sp, *3 tr in each sp to next corner 2-ch sp, (3 tr, 2 ch, 3 tr) in 2-ch sp; rep from * twice more, 3 tr in each sp to end, sl st to top of 3-ch, turn.

Round 6: as round 5 using yarn A.
Round 7: as round 5 using yarn F.
Round 8: as round 5 using yarn G.
Round 9: as round 5 using yarn A.
Round 10: as round 5 using yarn H.
Round 11: as round 5 using yarn I.
Round 12: as round 5 using yarn A.

You could line the bag with your favourite fabric to make it sturdier and more secure.

Small granny squares (make 40 in total)

These can be joined either by working in blo of each stitch or by using the continual joining method in round 3 (see page 136). Work the colour combinations as follows:

Square 1 (make 8)
Round 1: yarn C.
Round 2: yarn B.
Round 3: yarn A.

Square 2 (make 8)
Round 1: yarn F
Round 2: yarn D.
Round 3: yarn A.

Square 3 (make 8)
Round 1: yarn H.
Round 2: yarn E.
Round 3: yarn A.

Square 4 (make 8)
Round 1: yarn E.
Round 2: yarn C.
Round 3: yarn A.

Square 5 (make 8)
Round 1: yarn I.
Round 2: yarn G.
Round 3: yarn A.

Using suggested yarn, 4 ch, sl st to first ch to form ring.

Round 1 (RS): 3 ch (counts as 1 tr here and throughout) 2 tr in ring, 2 ch, (3 tr, 2 ch) three times in ring, join with sl st to top of 3-ch, turn. Change to next suggested yarn.
Round 2 (WS): 3 ch, (2 tr, 2 ch, 3 tr) in same 2-ch sp, (3 tr, 2 ch, 3 tr) in each 2-ch sp, sl st to join, turn. Change to yarn A.
Round 3: 2 ch, 2 htr in sp between 3-tr groups, (3 htr, 2 ch, 3 htr) in next 2-ch sp, *3 htr in next sp, (3 htr, 2 ch, 3 htr) in next 2-ch sp; rep from * twice more, sl st to top of 3-ch, turn.
Fasten off.

Joining

Using the schematic as a guide, join the granny squares as shown, working in a neat whip stitch around the three sides.

For a different look, why not try replacing the tassels with small – or even large – pom-poms?

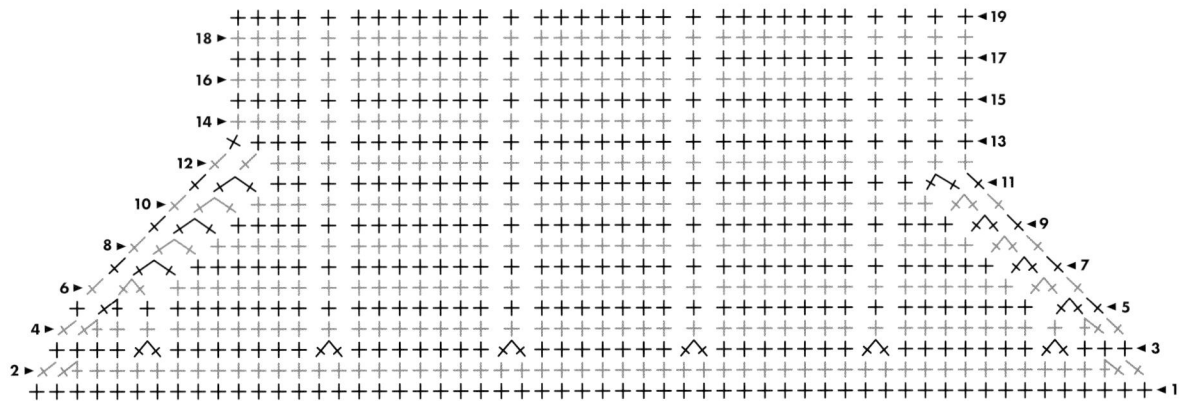

Top edge

Join yarn A in top corner of one
motif at seam edge.

Row 1 (RS): work 1 tr in corner sp,
work 1 tr in each htr to next corner
sp, miss corner sp, *miss corner sp
of next motif, work 1 dc in each
of 9 htr across top of square, miss
corner sp; rep from * along each
motif to end but working 1 dc in last
corner sp of last motif at seamed
edge, turn (56 sts).

Row 2: 1 dc in first dc, dc2tog, dc
to last 3 dc, dc2tog, 1 dc in last dc,
turn (54 sts).

Row 3: 3 dc, dc2tog, [7 dc,
dc2tog] to last 4 sts, 4 dc, turn
(48 sts).

Rows 3–11: rep row 2 (32 sts).
Fasten off, change to yarn C.

Rows 12–19: 1 dc in each st to
end, turn. Fasten off. Repeat on the
other side of the bag.

Finishing

Sew the handle into the folded top
section of the bag using a neat
whip stitch and allowing the work
to naturally curl around handle
Weave in yarn ends.

Tassels

Make three tassels using three
different coloured yarns.

1. Wrap the yarn around a 9cm
(3½in) piece of card twenty times.

2. Thread a 30cm (12in) piece of
yarn through the wrapped yarn and
tie at top.

3. Cut along the bottom of
the card.

4. Tie another length of yarn about
1cm (½in) down from the first tie at
the top.

5. Trim the tassels threads evenly.

6. Smooth the yarn in the tassels by
ironing on a low heat.

7. Plait the ends used to tie the top
of tassel together, then attach to the
bag near the handle.

Carnival Cowl

This cowl is simple to make and can be as bright as you like! It will warm you up as well as adding a pop of carnival colour to a winter outfit.

Tools and materials

Scheepjes Metropolis, 75% wool, 25% nylon
50g (1¾oz) = 200m (218yd)
Yarn A: Salvador 029 x 1 ball
Yarn B: Toulouse 030 x 1 ball
Yarn C: Washington 013 x 1ball
Yarn D: Marseille 019 x 1 ball
Yarn E: Johannesburg 054 x 1 ball

Yarn F: Bangalore 052 x 1 ball
Yarn G: Darwin 044 x 1 ball
Yarn H: Leeds 046 x 1 ball
Yarn I: Quebec 077 x 1 ball
Yarn J: Brasov 038 x 1 ball
Size 3.5mm (E/4) hook
Yarn needle

Yarn substitutes

Any 4-ply weight yarn would be a suitable substitute.

See also

• The classic granny square, page 14

A cowl is the perfect alternative to a scarf; scarves can be bulky and cumbersome under a coat or in your bag, which is not a problem with a cowl – a cowl will also work up much more quickly.

Schematic

The numbers next to the squares correspond to the colourway of that square.

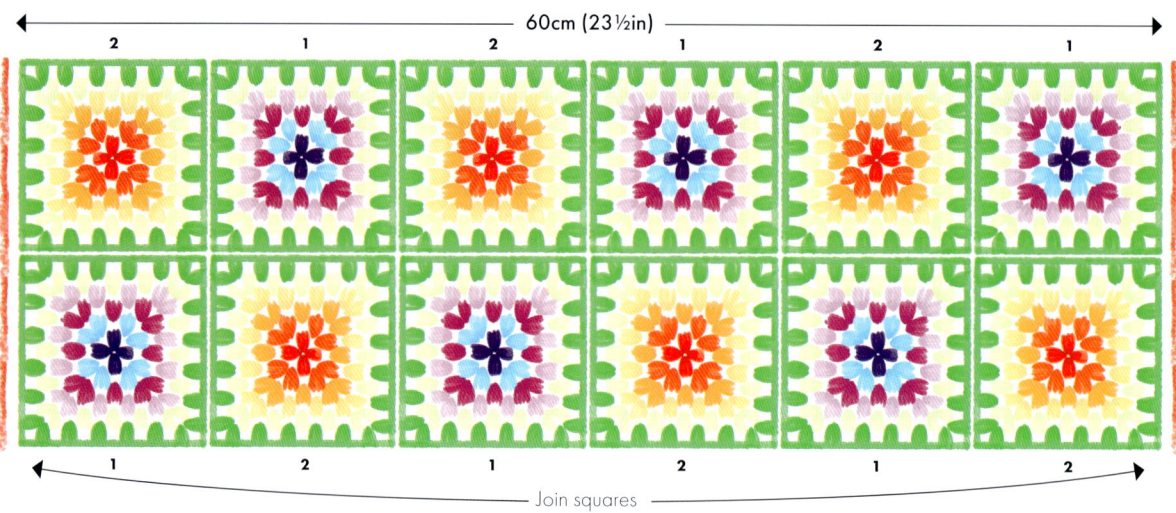

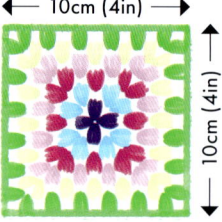

Tension

• Granny square measures 10 x 10cm (4 x 4in) using size 3.5mm (E/4) hook.

Special stitches (top and bottom cuff edging – see page 63)

• Front post treble crochet (fptr): Yrh, insert hook from front to back to front around vertical post of next stitch, yrh and draw up a loop, (3 loops on hook), yrh and draw through two loops, yrh and draw through next two loops to complete the stitch.

• Back post treble crochet (bptr): Yrh, insert hook from back to front to back around vertical post of next stitch, yrh and draw up a loop, (3 loops on hook), yrh and draw through two loops, yrh and draw through next two loops to complete the stitch.

Granny square (make 12 in total)

Square 1 (make 6)
Round 1: yarn C.
Round 2: yarn D.
Round 3: yarn E.
Round 4: yarn F.
Round 5: yarn B.
Round 6: yarn A.

Square 2 (make 6)
Round 1: yarn G.
Round 2: yarn H.
Round 3: yarn I.
Round 4: yarn J.
Round 5: yarn B.
Round 6: yarn A.

Using suggested yarn, 4 ch, sl st to first ch to form ring.

Round 1 (RS): 3 ch (counts as 1 tr here and throughout) 2 tr in ring, 2 ch, (3 tr, 2 ch) three times in ring, join with sl st to top of 3-ch, turn. Fasten off. Join next yarn in any corner 2-ch sp.

Round 2 (WS): 3 ch, (2 tr, 2 ch, 3 tr) in same 2-ch sp, (3 tr, 2 ch, 3 tr) in each 2-ch sp, sl st to join, turn. Fasten off. Join next yarn in any corner 2-ch sp.

Round 3: 3 ch, (2 tr, 2 ch, 3 tr) in same 2-ch sp, 3 tr in sp between 3-tr groups, *(3 tr, 2 ch, 3 tr) in next 2-ch sp, 3 tr in sp between 3-tr groups; rep from * twice more, sl st to top of 3-ch, turn.

Fasten off. Join next yarn in any corner 2-ch sp.

Round 4: 3 ch, (2 tr, 2 ch, 3 tr) in same 2-ch sp, 3 tr in sp between each 3-tr group to next corner 2-ch sp, *(3 tr, 2 ch, 3 tr) in next 2-ch sp, 3 tr in sp between each 3-tr group to next corner 2-ch sp; rep from * twice more, sl st to top of 30-ch, turn.

Fasten off. Join next yarn in any corner 2-ch sp.

Round 5: rep round 4.

Fasten off. Join yarn A in any corner 2-ch sp.

Round 6: as round 4.

Fasten off.

The brighter tones can be used to add a pop of colour to an otherwise muted winter palette.

The perfect winter accessory. Wear over your head or around your neck for two different looks.

You could pick a contrasting colour for the ribbing to make those colours really stand out.

Joining

Join the granny squares using the schematic as a guide. Round 6 can be used as a continual joining row (see page 136) or you can sew the squares together with a neat whip stitch.

Top and bottom cuff edging

Join yarn A in any st at top of cowl.
Set-up round: 1 ch (does not count as a st) work 1 dc in each st and ch-sp around, working an odd number of sts, sl st to join.
Round 1: 3 ch (counts as first tr), [1 fptr around next dc, 1 bptr around next dc] around, sl st to top of 3-ch to join, turn.

Round 2: 3 ch, [1 bptr, 1 fptr] around, sl st to join.
Fasten off.
Repeat on bottom edge of cowl.

To finish

Weave in yarn ends.

Sixties-Style Mini Dress

This beautiful dress will bring a swinging sixties vibe into your wardrobe, perfect for all the festival and garden party feels!

Tools and materials

Scheepjes Cotton 8 4ply, 100% cotton, 50g (1¾oz) = 170m (186yd)

Yarn A: Cobalt 519 x 8(9:9:12:13:13) balls

Yarn B: Violet 529 x 1(1:1:2:2:2) balls

Yarn C: Light Orange 639 x 1(1:1:2:2:2) balls

Yarn D: Light Turquoise 622 x 1(1:1:2:2:2) balls

Yarn E: Turquoise 712 x 1(1:1:2:2:2) balls

Yarn F: Canary 714 x 1(1:1:2:2:2) balls

Yarn G: Pink 719 x 1(1:1:2:2:2) balls

Yarn H: Fuchsia 720 x 1(1:1:2:2:2) balls

Yarn I: Orange 716 x 1(1:1:2:2:2) balls

Yarn J: Orange Pink 650 x 1(1:1:2:2:2) balls

Yarn K: Olive 669 x 1(1:1:2:2:2) balls

Yarn L: Sea Green 723 x 1(1:1:2:2:2) balls

Size 2.5mm (C/2) hook

Yarn needle

Yarn substitutes

Any 4-ply weight yarn would be a suitable substitute.

See also

• The turned granny square, page 16

Made from 100 per cent
cotton, this dress can be
worn in summer or in winter
if paired with tights.
It is strong and durable and
its soft fabric is kind to skin.

Sizes

	1	2	3	4	5	6	
To fit chest	81–86	91	97–101	107–112	117	122	cm
	32–34	36	38–40	42–44	46	48	in
Actual chest	96	104	112	120	128	136	cm
	37¾	41	44	47¼	50½	53½	in
Length	74	74	74	80	80	80	cm
	29¼	29¼	29¼	31½	31½	31½	in

The dress can be made in two lengths. The sample shown here has a slight crop but for a longer dress, you can add an extra row of squares along the bottom of the garment. But remember that this will require more yarn than stated. Garment size can also be adjusted by adding or subtracting widening rows. Each widening row will add approximately 1cm (½in) in width. Be sure to work the same number of widening rows on each side. There is an overall difference of 4cm (1½in) per size.

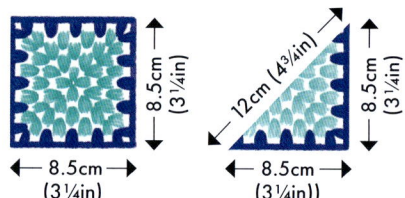

Tension

- Each square measures 8.5 x 8.5cm (3¼ x 3¼in) and 12cm (4¾in) across the diagonal.

Make the following number of squares in the eleven different colours:

Colours	B	C	D	E	F	G	H	I	J	K	L
Full squares: Size 1 to 3	10	9	10	8	9	9	10	9	7	9	9
Half squares: Size 1 to 3	5	6	6	6	6	7	5	6	5	5	5
Full squares: Size 4 to 6	13	13	14	12	13	12	13	13	10	14	13
Half squares: Size 4 to 6	2	6	7	7	9	9	6	6	7	6	3
Quarter squares: Size 4 to 6	-	-	-	-	1	-	-	1	1	-	1

Schematic

Squares are placed in random colour order. Use the schematic as a guide or freestyle your own colourways.

Sizes 1 to 3

Make 99 full squares and 62 half squares.

FRONT

BACK

SLEEVE

74cm (29¼in)

48cm (19in)
before widening rows

48cm (19in)
before widening rows

36cm (14¼in)
length before cuff rows

Sizes 4 to 6

Make 141 full squares, 68 half squares and four quarter squares.

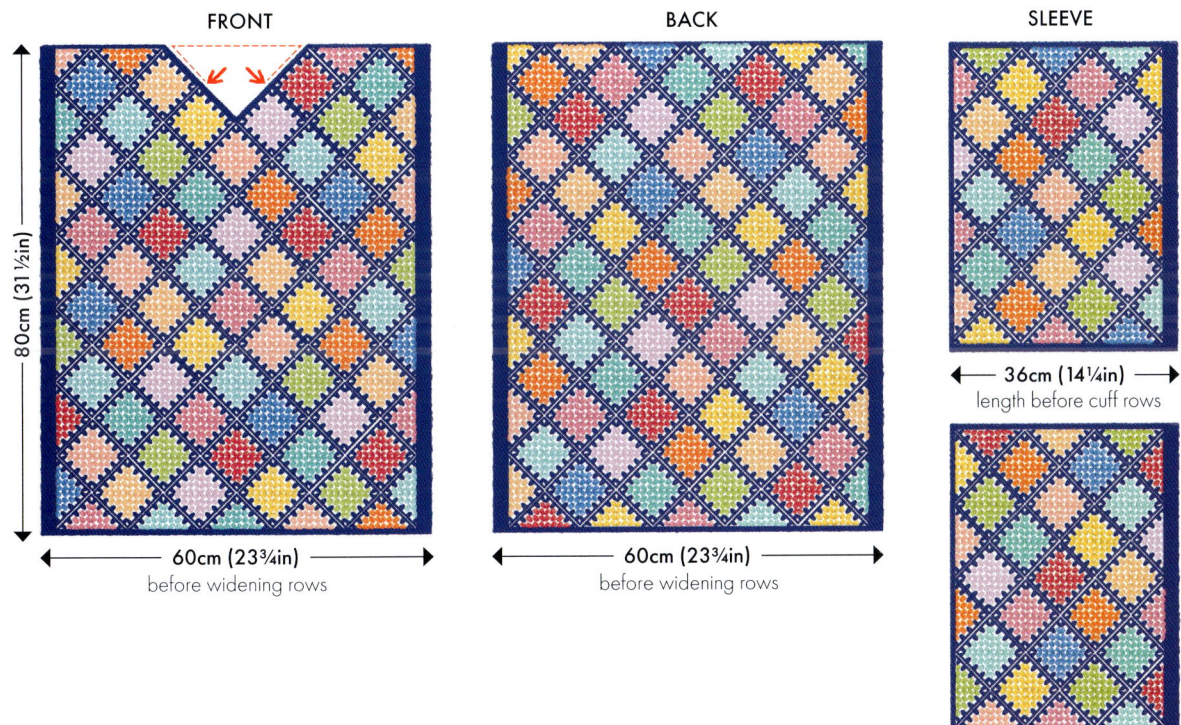

FRONT

BACK

SLEEVE

80cm (31½in)

60cm (23¾in)
before widening rows

60cm (23¾in)
before widening rows

36cm (14¼in)
length before cuff rows

Full square (make 99 for sizes 1–3 and 141 for sizes 4–6)

Turn at the end of each round throughout.

Using yarns B–K and a size 2.5mm (C/2) hook, 4 ch, sl st to first ch to form a ring.

Round 1: 3 ch (counts as 1 tr here and throughout), 2 tr, 2 ch, (3 tr, 2 ch) three times in ring, sl st to join, turn.

Round 2: sl st in corner 2-ch sp, 3 ch, (2 tr, 2 ch, 3 tr) in same corner 2-ch sp, (3 tr, 2 ch, 3 tr) in each corner 2-ch sp, sl st to join, turn.

Round 3: sl st in space between 3-tr groups, 3 ch, 2 tr in same sp, (3 tr, 2 ch, 3 tr) in next corner 2-ch sp, *3 tr in space between 3-tr groups, (3 tr, 2 ch, 3 tr) in corner 2-ch sp; rep from * twice more, sl st to join, turn.

Round 4: sl st to space between 3-tr groups, 3 ch, 2 tr in same sp, (3 tr, 2 ch, 3 tr) in corner 2-ch sp, *3 tr in each of next two sps between 3-tr groups, (3 tr, 2 ch, 3 tr) in next corner 2-ch sp; rep from * twice more, 3 tr in space before last 3-tr group, sl st to join, turn. Fasten off. Join yarn A in any corner 2-ch sp.

Round 5: 3 ch, (2 tr, 2 ch, 3 tr) in same corner 2-ch sp, 3 tr in space between each 3-tr group to next corner, *(3 tr, 2 ch, 3 tr) in corner 2-ch sp, 3 tr in space between each 3-tr group to next corner; rep from * twice more, sl st to join.

Note: Use the continual joining method (see page 136) with round 5, using the schematic as a guide or proceed as follows if the individual squares are to be sewn together.

Half square (make 62 for sizes 1–3 and 68 for sizes 4–6)

Using yarns B–K and a size 2.5mm (C/2) hook, 4 ch, sl st to first ch to form a ring.

Row 1: 4 ch (counts as 1 tr and 1 ch here and throughout), (3 tr, 2 ch, 3 tr, 1 ch, 1 tr) all in ring, turn.

Row 2: 4 ch, 3 tr in 1-ch sp, (3 tr, 2 ch, 3 tr) in corner 2-ch sp, 3 tr in 1-ch sp, 1 ch 1 tr in third of 4-ch, turn.

Row 3: 4 ch, 3 tr in 1-ch sp, 3 tr in space between 3-tr groups, (3 tr, 2 ch, 3 tr) in corner 2-ch sp, 3 tr in space between 3-tr groups, 3 tr in 1-ch sp, 1 ch, 1 tr in third of 4-ch, turn.

Row 4: 4 ch, 3 tr in 1-ch sp, 3 tr in space between 3-tr groups to corner 2-ch sp, (3 tr, 2 ch, 3 tr) in corner 2-ch sp, 3 tr in space between 3-tr groups to end, 3 tr in 1-ch sp, 1 ch, 1 tr in third of 4-ch, turn. Fasten off. Join yarn A in top of last tr.

Row 5: rep round 4. Fasten off.

The half squares make up the outside edges of each panel (front, back and sleeves).

Quarter square

(make four for sizes 4 and 5 ONLY)

Using chosen yarn and a size 2.5mm (C/2) hook, 4 ch, sl st to first ch to form a ring.

Row 1: 3 ch (counts as first tr) (2 tr, 2 ch, 3 tr) in ring, turn.

Row 2: 3 ch, (3 tr, 2 ch, 3 tr) in corner 2-ch sp, 1 tr in third of beg 3-ch, turn.

Row 3: 3 ch, 1 tr in space before first 3-tr group, (3 tr, 2 ch, 3 tr) in corner 2-ch sp, 1 tr in space before last tr, 1 tr in top of 3-ch, turn.

Row 4: 3 ch, 3 tr in space before first 3-tr group, (3 tr, 2 ch, 3 tr) in corner 2-ch sp, 3 tr in space before last 2 tr, 1 tr in top of 3-ch, turn.

Fasten off. Join yarn A in top of last tr.

Row 5: 3 ch, 1 tr in space before first 3-tr group, 3 tr in space between 3-tr groups, (3 tr, 2 ch, 3 tr) in corner 2-ch sp, 3 tr in space between 3-tr groups, 1 tr in space before last tr, 1 tr in last tr.

Fasten off.

To join

If you are not using the continual joining method, sew the squares together using yarn A and following the schematic using a neat whip stitch.

The dress is shown here in a cropped length, but you can make it longer by adding another row of squares.

Body widening rows

(sizes 2, 3, 5 and 6 ONLY)

Rejoin yarn A to a corner of one long edge of the front.

Row 1: 3 ch (counts as first tr), work 2 tr under each row end and 1 tr in each 4 ch at centre of squares to end of row, turn (–[126:26:–:137:137]) sts.

Row 2: 3 ch, tr to end, turn.

Rep row 2 a further –(0:2:–:0:2) times.

Fasten off.

Repeat along remaining three long edges of body pieces.

Cotton yarn is not as
stretchy as other yarns, so
make sure you check your
measurements carefully.

Sleeve widening rows

(sizes 2, 3, 5 and 6 ONLY)

Rejoin yarn A to one corner of the sleeve, on sizes 5 and 6 join to corner of short edge.
Row 1: 3 ch (counts as first tr), work 2 tr under each row end and 1 tr in each 4 ch at centre of squares to end of row, turn (63 sts).

Sizes 3 and 6 only
Row 2: 3 ch, tr to end, turn.
Fasten off.
Repeat on opposite sleeve edge.

To make up

Join front panel to the back panel at the shoulder.

Fold the sleeve in half lengthways, matching the halfway point to the shoulder seam and with the sleeve widening rows meeting at the underarm. Sew in place and sew the side seam and sleeve seams.

Bottom edging

Join yarn A into the side seam at the bottom of the garment.
Row 1: 1 ch (does not count as a st), work dc under each row end and 1 dc in each 4-ch at centre of squares around, sl st to join, turn.
Rows 2–6: 1 ch, dc around, sl st to join, turn.
Fasten off.

Cuffs

Join yarn A at the sleeve seam of cuff edge.
Work 4 rounds in dc as for bottom edging.
Fasten off.

Collar

Join yarn A at the back of the neck.
Round 1: 1 ch (does not counts as a st), work 2 dc under each row end and 1 dc in each 4-ch at centre of squares around neck opening, sl st to join.
Fasten off.
Rejoin yarn at point marked with red arrow on schematic.
Row 1: 3 ch (counts as first tr), 1 tr in each dc around neck opening to second red arrow.

Row 2: 3 ch, tr to end, turn.
Rows 3–6: 3 ch, 3 tr in next st, 1 tr in each st to last 2 sts, 3 tr in next st, 1 tr, turn.
Fasten off.
Rejoin yarn at back of neck, work in dc around entire collar and v neck working 1 dc in each tr and 2 dc in each row end, sl st to join.
Fasten off.
Weave in all yarn ends.

Lightly block or steam the collar at the end to give a sharp finish.

Half & Half Jumper

The half-and-half squares used in this jumper echo the shapes used in Moroccan tiles. You can use any combination of different colours to make it suit your style.

Tools and materials

Scheepjes Merino Soft DK, 25% microfibre, 50% wool, 25% acrylic 50g (1¾oz) = 105m (115yd)

Yarn A: Raphael 602 x 14(15:16:17:17) balls

Yarn B: Pollock 601 x 1(1:1:2:2) balls

Yarn C: Monet 639 x 1(1:1:2:2) balls

Yarn D: Bellini 654 x 1(1:1:2:2) balls

Yarn E: Degas 632 x 1(1:1:2:2) balls

Yarn F: Soutine 615 x 1(1:1:2:2) balls

Yarn G: Magritte 614 x 1(1:1:2:2) balls

Yarn H: Van Eych 645 x 1(1:1:2:2) balls

Yarn I: Caravaggio 642 x 1(1:1:2:2) balls

Yarn J: Warhol 640 x 1(1:1:2:2) balls

Yarn K: Matisse 635 x 1(1:1:2:2) balls

Yarn L: Miro 646 x 1(1:1:2:2) balls
Size 4mm (G/6) hook
Yarn needle

Yarn substitutes

Any DK weight yarn would be a suitable substitute.

See also

• The diagonal granny square, page 19

Tuck the jumper into a pair of jeans for an everyday look or a pair of suit trousers to elevate the outfit and wear it to the office.

Special stitches

- Front post treble crochet (fptr): yrh, insert hook from front to back to front around vertical post of next stitch, yrh and draw up a loop, (3 loops on hook), yrh and draw through 2 loops, yrh and draw through next 2 loops to complete the stitch.

- Back post treble crochet (bptr): yrh, insert hook from back to front to back around vertical post of next stitch, yrh and draw up a loop, (3 loops on hook), yrh and draw through 2 loops, yrh and draw through next 2 loops to complete the stitch.

Sizes and schematic

To fit	1	2	3	4	5	
Actual chest	110	120	130	140	148	cm
	43¼	47¼	51¼	55¼	58¼	in
Length to shoulder	63	68	73	78	78	cm
	24¼	26¾	28¾	30¾	30¾	in
Sleeve length	43	43	43	44	44	cm
	17	17	17	17¼	17¼	in

Tension

- One half-and-half granny square measures 11(12:13:14:14) x 11(12:13:14:14)cm (4¼ [4¾:5¼:5½:5½] x 4¼ [4¾:5¼:5½:5½]in) using size 4mm (G/6) hook, before blocking.

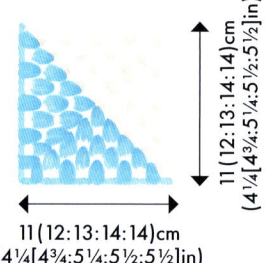

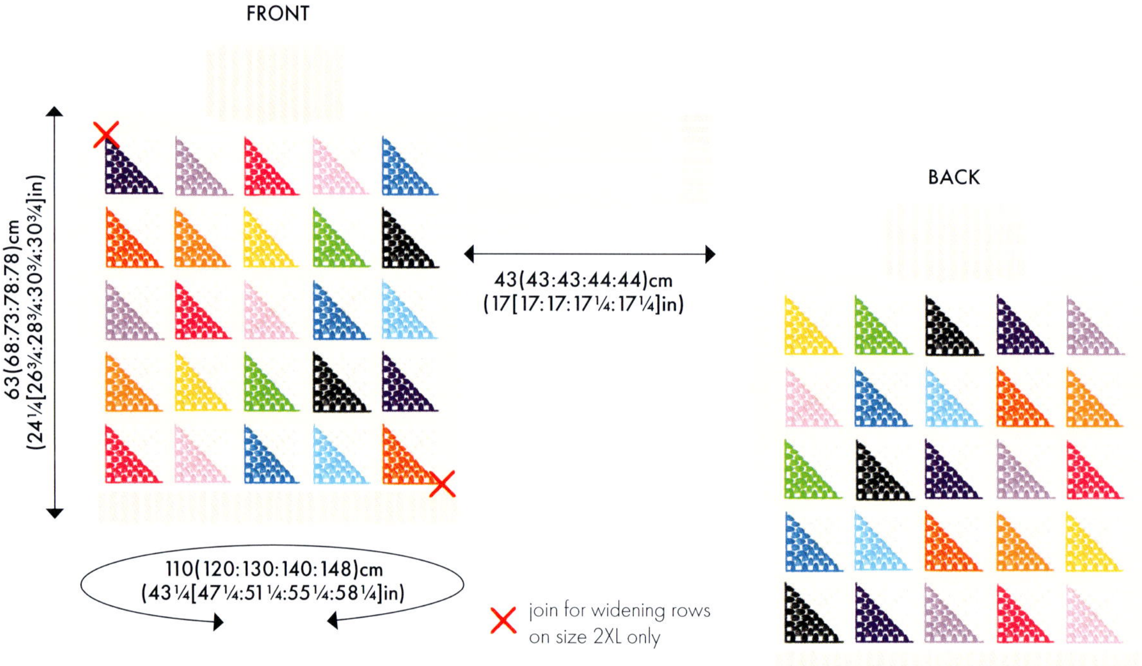

11(12:13:14:14)cm
(4¼[4¾:5¼:5½:5½]in)

11(12:13:14:14)cm
(4¼[4¾:5¼:5½:5½]in)

FRONT

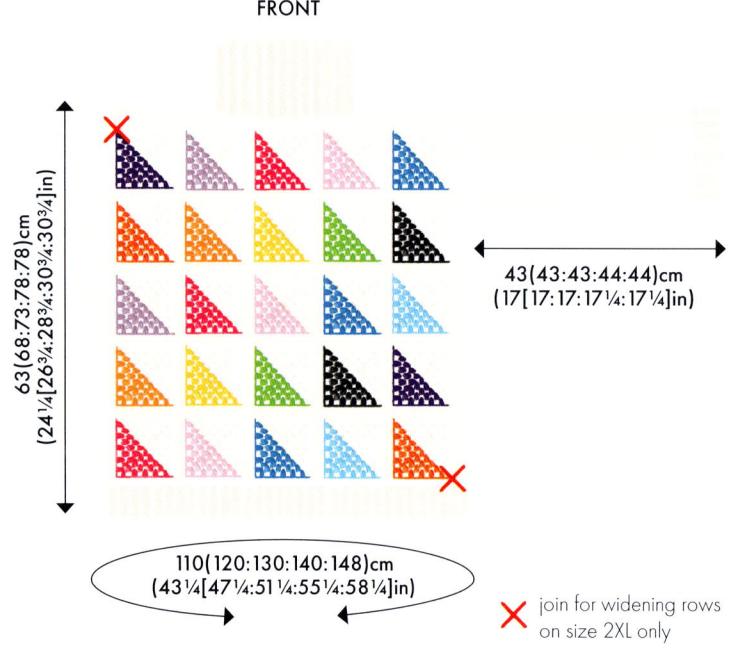

63(68:73:78:78)cm
(24¼[26¾:28¾:30¾:30¾]in)

43(43:43:44:44)cm
(17[17:17:17¼:17¼]in)

110(120:130:140:148)cm
(43¼[47¼:51¼:55¼:58¼]in)

✕ join for widening rows on size 2XL only

BACK

Make the following number of squares in the eleven different colours along with yarn A. Or choose your own colour combinations. See size information in the pattern for number of rows per square:

Colours	B	C	D	E	F	G	H	I	J	K	L
Number of squares	5	5	5	5	5	4	4	4	4	5	4

Half-and-half granny square (make 50 in total)

For front and back sections make 50 squares in total. The half-and-half square is made in two colours. Use yarn A and any of the other colours listed, using the schematic as a guide, or use scraps from your DK stash and create your own colour pattern. Do not work over the contrasting colour; leave it hanging where you finish, ready to be picked up on the next round.

Using first colour, 4 ch, sl st to first ch to form a ring.
Round 1: 3 ch (counts as 1 tr here and throughout), (2 tr, 2 ch, 3 tr) in ring, 1 ch, pick up second colour and work 1 ch, (3 tr, 2 ch, 3 tr) all in ring, 2 ch, sl st in third of beg 3-ch, turn.
Cont with second colour.
Round 2: sl st in corner 2-ch sp, (3 ch, 2 tr) in corner 2-ch sp, (3 tr, 2 ch, 3 tr) in next corner 2-ch sp, 3 tr in next corner 2-ch sp, 1 ch, pick up first colour, 1 ch, 3 tr in same corner 2-ch sp, (3 tr, 2 ch, 3 tr) in next corner 2-ch sp, 3 tr in first corner 2-ch sp, 2 ch, sl st in third of

beg 3-ch, turn.
Cont with first colour.
Round 3: sl st in corner 2-ch sp, (3 ch, 2 tr) in same 2-ch sp, 3 tr in space between 3-tr groups, (3 tr, 2 ch, 3 tr) in next corner 2-ch sp, 3 tr in space between 3-tr groups, 3 tr in next corner 2-ch sp, 1 ch, change to second colour, 1 ch, 3 tr in same corner 2-ch sp, 3 tr in space between 3-tr groups, (3 tr, 2 ch, 3 tr) in next corner 2-ch sp, 3 tr in space between 3-tr groups, 3 tr in first corner 2-ch sp, 2 ch, sl st in third of beg 3-ch, turn.
Cont with second colour.
Round 4: sl st in corner 2-ch sp, (3 ch, 2 tr) in same 2-ch sp, 3 tr in space between each 3-tr group to corner, (3 tr, 2 ch, 3 tr) in 2-ch sp, 3 tr in space between each 3-tr group to corner, 3 tr in 2-ch sp, 1 ch, change to first colour, 1 ch, 3 tr in same corner 2-ch sp, 3 tr in space between 3-tr groups to corner, (3 tr, 2 ch, 3 tr) in 2-ch sp, 3 tr in space between 3-tr groups to first corner, 3 tr in 2-ch sp, 2 ch, sl st in third of beg 3-ch, turn.

Cont with first colour.
Round 5: sl st in corner 2-ch sp, (3 ch, 2 tr) in same 2-ch sp, 3 tr in space between each 3-tr group to corner, (3 tr, 2 ch, 3 tr) in 2-ch sp, 3 tr in space between each 3-tr group to corner, 3 tr in 2-ch sp, 1 ch, change to second colour, 1 ch, 3 tr in same corner 2-ch sp, 3 tr in space between 3-tr groups to corner, (3 tr, 2 ch, 3 tr) in 2-ch sp, 3 tr in space between 3-tr groups to first corner, 3 tr in 2-ch sp, 2 ch, sl st in third of beg 3-ch, turn.

Size 1 only
Fasten off.

Size 2 only
Cont with second colour.
Round 6: sl st in corner 2-ch sp, 1 ch, 1 dc in same 2-ch sp, 1 dc in each tr to next corner 2-ch sp, (1 dc, 2 ch, 1 dc) in corner 2-ch sp, 1 dc in each tr to next corner 2-ch sp, 1 dc in corner 2-ch sp, 1 ch, change to first colour, 1 ch, 1 dc in same corner 2-ch sp, 1 dc in each tr to next corner 2-ch sp, (1 dc,

Squares are placed in random colour order. Use the schematic as a guide or freestyle your own colourways.

2 ch, 1 dc) in corner 2-ch sp, 1 dc in each st to first corner sp, sl st first ch.
Fasten off.

Sizes 3, 4 and 5 only
Cont with second colour.
Round 6: sl st in corner 2-ch sp, (3 ch, 2 tr) in same 2-ch sp, 3 tr in space between each 3-tr group to corner, (3 tr, 2 ch, 3 tr) in 2-ch sp, 3 tr in space between each 3-tr group to corner, 3 tr in 2-ch sp, 1 ch, change to first colour, 1 ch, 3 tr in same corner 2-ch sp, 3 tr in space between 3-tr groups to corner, (3 tr, 2 ch, 3 tr) in 2-ch sp, 3 tr in space between 3-tr groups to first corner, 3 tr in 2-ch sp, 2 ch, sl st in third of beg 3-ch, turn.
Size 3 fasten off.

Sizes 4 and 5 only
Cont with first colour.
Round 7: sl st in corner 2-ch sp, 1 ch, 1 dc in same 2-ch sp, 1 dc in each tr to next corner 2-ch sp, (1 dc, 2 ch, 1 dc) in corner 2-ch sp, 1 dc in each tr to next corner 2-ch sp, 1 dc in corner 2-ch sp, 1 ch, change to second colour, 1 ch, 1 dc in same corner 2-ch sp, 1 dc in each tr to next corner 2-ch sp, (1 dc, 2 ch, 1 dc) in corner 2-ch sp, 1 dc in each st to first corner sp, 1 dc, 1 ch in corner sp, sl st in first ch.
Fasten off.

The high neck design of this jumper means there is a higher risk of picking up cosmetics from the neck and face during the day. See page 138 to learn how to remove stains from your crochet garments.

Assemble front and back panels

Now join the squares for the front and back panels, using a neat whip stitch, as shown on the schematic before working the sleeves.

Widening rows

Size 5 only
Work widening rows at each side edge of front and back panels as follows.
Join yarn A (or colour of choice) into corner 2-ch sp (indicated with a red cross on the schematic).
Row 1: 3 ch (counts as 1 tr), 1 tr in same ch sp, now work 1 tr in each st, 1 tr in each ch sp and 2 tr in final 2-ch sp along, turn.
Row 2: 3 ch, tr to end.
Fasten off.
Repeat on opposite side.

Although the sleeves are not made of granny squares, they are easy to make with rows of treble crochets.

Shoulder shaping

Sizes 1, 2, 3 and 4 only
Work the back and the front alike.

First side
Row 1: join yarn A in corner ch sp, 3 ch (counts as 1 tr), 1 tr in each of next 24(25:27:29:–) sts counting each corner ch sp as 1 st, turn (25[26:28:30:–] sts).
Row 2: 3 ch, tr to end, turn.
Row 3: 3 ch, tr to end, fasten off.

Second side
Join yarn A, 25(26:28:30:–) sts in from opposite edge.
Row 1: 3 ch (counts as 1 tr), 1 tr in each of next 24(25:27:29:–) sts counting each corner ch sp as 1 st, turn (25[26:28:30:–] sts).
Row 2: 3 ch, tr to end, turn.
Row 3: 3 ch, tr to end, fasten off.

Size 5 only
Work the back and the front alike.

First side
Row 1: join yarn A under first row end of widening row, 3 ch, (counts as 1 tr), work 1 more tr under same row, 2 tr under next row then work 29 tr counting each corner ch sp as 1 st, turn (33 sts).
Row 2: 3 ch, tr to end, turn.
Row 3: 3 ch, tr to end, fasten off.

Second side
Join yarn A 30 sts in from opposite edge (not counting widening rows).
Row 1: 3 ch (counts as 1 tr), 1 tr in each of next 28 sts counting each corner ch sp as 1 st, turn, 2 tr under each of next 2 widening row ends (33 sts).
Row 2: 3 ch, tr to end, turn.
Row 3: 3 ch, tr to end, fasten off.

Sleeves

Work both sleeves in the same way.

Cuff
Using yarn C, 11 ch.
Row 1: 1 dc in second ch from hook and in each ch to end, turn (10 dc).
Rows 2–32(32:34:36:38): 1 ch (does not count as a st), dc blo in each st to end, turn.
Fasten off.
Using yarn A, work along the long edge of cuff as follows:
Row 1: work 32(32:34:36:38)dc along long edge, turn.
Row 2: 3 ch (counts as first tr), 1 tr in same st, 1 tr in each st to last st, 2 tr in last st, turn (34 [34:36:38:40]tr).
Rows 3 and 4: rep row 2 (38[38:40:42:44]tr).
Rows 5 and 6: 3 ch, 1 tr in each st to end, turn.
Row 7: rep row 2 (40[40:42:44:46]tr).

Sizes 1, 2 and 3 only

Rows 8–28: rep rows 5–7 seven times (54[54:56:–:–] sts).

Rows 29–31: 3 ch, 1 tr in each st to end, turn.

Rows 32–34: 3 ch, 1 tr in each st to end, fasten off.

Size 4 only

Rows 8–31: rep rows 5–7 eight times (60 sts).

Rows 32–34: 3 ch, 1 tr in each st to end, turn.

Row 35: 3 ch, 1 tr in each st to end, fasten off.

Size 5 only

Rows 8–35: rep rows 5–7 nine times (64 sts).

Fasten off.

To make up

Using whip stitch, sew up the side seams, leaving a gap for the sleeves. Sew shoulder seams.

Welt

Set-up round: join yarn A to side seam at bottom edge of garment, 1 ch (does not count as a st), work around entire bottom edge working 2 dc under each row end of widening rows on larger sizes and 1 dc in each tr, (do not work in ch sps), 9 ch, turn.

Row 1: 1 dc in second ch from hook and in each of next 7 ch, sl st in next dc of main round, sl st in foll dc, turn.

Row 2: tr blo to end, 1 ch, turn.

Row 3: tr blo to end, sl st in next st of main round, sl st in foll st, turn.

Rep rows 2 and 3 around entire bottom edge of garment.

Fasten off.

Rollneck

Join yarn A at left shoulder seam.

Round 1: 1 ch (does not count as a st) work in dc evenly around neck opening, working an even number of sts, sl st to first dc to join.

Round 2: 3 ch (counts as first st), 1 tr in each dc around.

Round 3: 3 ch, 1 bptr around next st, [1 fptr, 1 bptr] around sl st to join.

Rounds 4–24(26:27:28:28): Rep round 3.

Fasten off.

Finishing

Weave in yarn ends.

Block lightly.

Place a small stay stitch at each side of the neck to keep the rollneck in place.

Summer Nights Wrap

Wrap yourself up in this colourful shawl! When day turns into night, it's the perfect addition to any summer outfit.

Tools and materials

Scheepjes Catona 4ply 100% cotton
50g (1¾oz) = 125m (137yd)
Yarn A: Bridal White 105 x 4 balls
Yarn B: Tulip 222 x 3 balls
Yarn C: Vivid Blue 146 x 3 balls
Yarn D: Apple Granny 513 x 3 balls
Yarn E: Shocking Pink 114 x 3 balls
Yarn F: Rich Coral 410 x 3 balls
Yarn G: Lemon 280 x 3 balls
Size 4mm (G/6) hook

Yarn substitutes

Any 4-ply weight yarn would be a suitable substitute

See also

• The classic granny square, page 14

There are so many ways to wear this wrap! Simply throw around your shoulders or wrap around your neck and make a real statement.

Schematic

The numbers next to the squares correspond to the colourway of that square.

Tension

- Small granny square measures 8.5 x 8.5cm (3¼ x 3¼in)
- Large granny square measures 51 x 51cm (20 x 20in)
- Both made using size 4mm (G/6) hook or size required to obtain the correct tension.

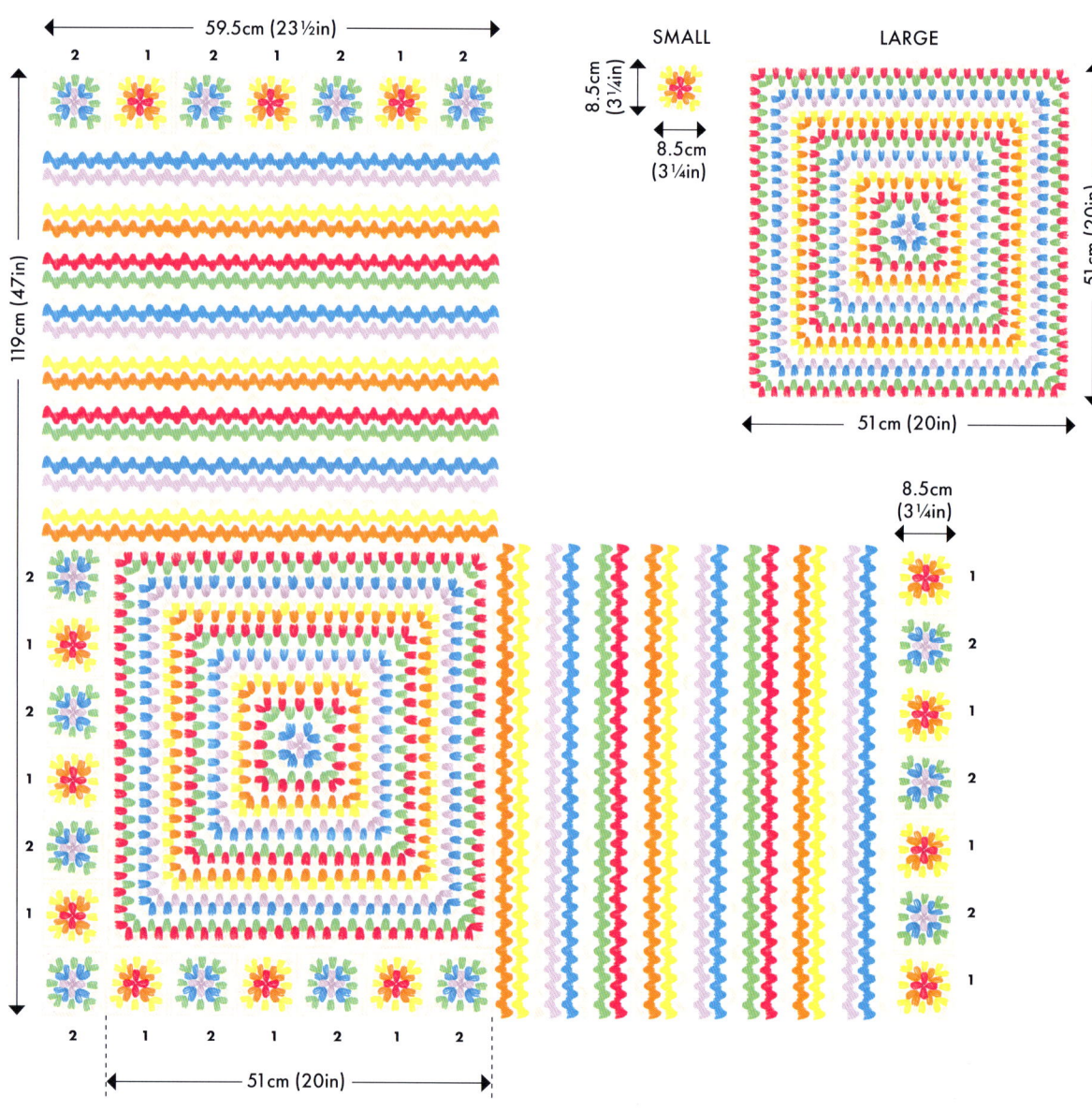

Large granny square (make one)

Using yarn B and a size 4mm (G/6) hook, 4 ch, sl st to first ch to form ring being careful not to twist sts.

Round 1 (RS): 3 ch (counts as 1 tr here and throughout) 2 tr in ring, 2 ch, (3 tr, 2 ch) three times in ring, join with sl st to top of 3-ch, turn. Fasten off yarn B. Join yarn C in corner 2-ch sp.

Round 2 (WS): 3 ch, (2 tr, 2 ch, 3 tr) in same 2-ch sp, (3 tr, 2 ch, 3 tr) in each of next three 2-ch sps, sl st to join, turn.

Fasten off yarn C. Join yarn A in corner 2-ch sp.

Round 3: 3 ch, (2 tr, 2 ch, 3 tr) in same 2-ch sp, 3 tr in sp before next 3-tr group, *(3 tr, 2 ch, 3 tr) in next 2-ch sp, 3 tr in sp before next 3-tr group; rep from * twice more, sl st to top of 3-ch, turn.

Fasten off yarn A. Join yarn D in corner 2-ch sp.

Round 4: 3 ch, (2 tr, 2 ch, 3 tr) in same 2-ch sp, 3 tr in sp before next two 3-tr groups, *(3 tr, 2 ch, 3 tr) in next 2-ch sp, 3 tr in sp before next two 3-tr groups; rep from * twice more, sl st to top of 3-ch, turn.

Fasten off yarn D. Join yarn E in corner 2-ch sp.

Round 5: 3 ch, (2 tr, 2 ch, 3 tr) in same 2-ch sp, 3 tr in each sp between 3-tr groups to next corner, *(3 tr, 2 ch, 3 tr) in next 2-ch sp, 3 tr in sp between each 3-tr group to next corner; rep from * twice more, sl st to top of 3-ch, turn.

Fasten off yarn E. Join yarn A in corner 2-ch sp.

Round 6: as round 5.

Round 7: as round 5 using yarn F.

Round 8: as round 5 using yarn G.

Round 9: as round 5 using yarn A.

Round 10: as round 5 using yarn B.

Round 11: as round 5 using yarn C.

Round 12: as round 5 using yarn A.

Round 13: as round 5 using yarn D.

Round 14: as round 5 using yarn E.

Round 15: as round 5 using yarn A.

Round 16: as round 5 using yarn F.

Round 17: as round 5 using yarn G.

Round 18: as round 5 using yarn A.

Round 19: as round 5 using yarn B.

Round 20: as round 5 using yarn C.

Round 21: as round 5 using yarn A.

Round 22: as round 5 using yarn D.

Round 23: as round 5 using yarn E.

Round 24: as round 5 using yarn A.

Small granny squares (make 27 in total)

Work as for rounds 1–4 of Large granny square using following yarn colours:

Square 1 (make 13)
Round 1: yarn E.
Round 2: yarn F.
Round 3: yarn G.
Round 4: yarn A.

Square 2 (make 14)
Round 1: yarn B.
Round 2: yarn C.
Round 3: yarn D.
Round 4: yarn A.

Always ensure your granny squares stay square and sharp by turning each row, then blocking lightly before joining.

Joining

Join a row of six squares along the bottom edge of the Large granny square, then join seven squares down the adjoining side (see schematic). Use whip stitch to join, placing the squares right side to right side.

GRANNY STITCH IN ROWS

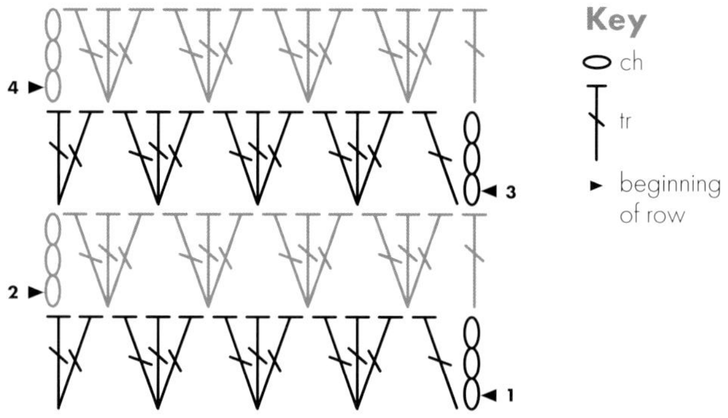

Rows 2 & 3 repeated from pattern

Key

○ ch

† tr

► beginning of row

Side panels (see Granny Stitch chart above)

Work both panels in the same way. With RS facing, rejoin yarn F in corner ch sp of one unworked edge of the Large granny square.

Row 1: 3 ch, 1 tr in same sp, 3 tr in each space between 3-tr groups to end of row, (Note: The space between a small square and large square counts as 1 space), work 2 tr in last st, turn (27 x 3-tr groups with 2 tr at each end).
Row 2: 3 ch (counts as first tr), miss 1 tr, 3 tr in each sp between 3-tr groups to last 2 sts, miss 1 tr, 1 tr in top of 3-ch, turn.
Change to yarn G.
Row 3: 3 ch, 1 tr in same st,

miss next 3 tr, 3 tr in each space between 3-tr groups to last 3-tr group, miss last 3-tr group and work 2 tr in 3 ch, turn.
Row 4: 3 ch, miss 1 tr, 3 tr in each sp between 3-tr groups to last 2 sts, miss 1 tr, 1 tr in top of 3-ch, turn.
Rows 3 and 4 form the pattern rows and are repeated.
Continue in pattern as set, working colours as follows:
Rows 5 and 6: using yarn A.
Rows 7 and 8: using yarn B.
Rows 9 and 10: using yarn C.
Rows 11 and 12: using yarn A.
Rows 13 and 14: using yarn D.
Rows 15 and 16: using yarn E.
Rows 17 and 18: using yarn A.

Rows 19–36: work in pattern, repeating colour sequence of previous 18 rows.
Rows 37–48: rep rows 1–12 of colour sequence.
Fasten off.

Finishing

Use the remaining 14 squares to join seven squares to each short end of the wrap, using whip stitch to join. Using yarn A, work two rows of dc around the entire wrap. Fasten off and sew in yarn ends.

The perfect garment to stave off the winter chill; throw over your favourite dress, and dance the night away.

Kaleidoscope Jumper

This on-trend top with baggy fit sleeves is perfect for everyday wear. And crocheting colourful round after colourful round makes this such a therapeutic project to make!

Tools and materials

Scheepjes Metropolis, 75% merino wool, 25% nylon
50g (1¾oz) = 200m (218yd)
Yarn A: Bucharest 001 x 2(3:3:4:4:5) balls
Yarn B: Perth 045 x 2(2:2:2:2:3) balls
Yarn C: Bangalore 052 x 2(2:2:2:2:3) balls
Yarn D: Brasov 038 x 2(2:2:2:2:3) balls

Yarn E: Quebec 077 x 2(2:2:2:2:3) balls
Yarn F: Lima 055 x 1(2:2:2:2:3) balls
Yarn G: Lahore 014 x 1(1:2:2:2:3) balls
Yarn H: Salvadore 029 x 1(1:2:2:2:3) balls
Size 3.5mm (E/4) hook
Yarn needle

Yarn substitutes

Any DK weight yarn that works to the same tension would be a suitable substitute.

See also

• The classic granny square, page 14

The piece is created in a kaleidoscope of colours, which means you can pair it with a whole range of items in your wardrobe. Here it is paired with green trousers, similar in shade to the green yarn (H) used for the jumper.

Sizes and schematic

To fit	1	2	3	4	5	6	
Actual chest	100	108	116	124	132	140	cm
	39½	42½	45¾	48¾	52	55¼	in
Length	58	62	66	70	70	70	cm
	23	24½	26	27½	27½	27½	in
Sleeve length	48	48	49.5	49.5	50	50	cm
	19	19	19½	19½	19¾	19¾	in

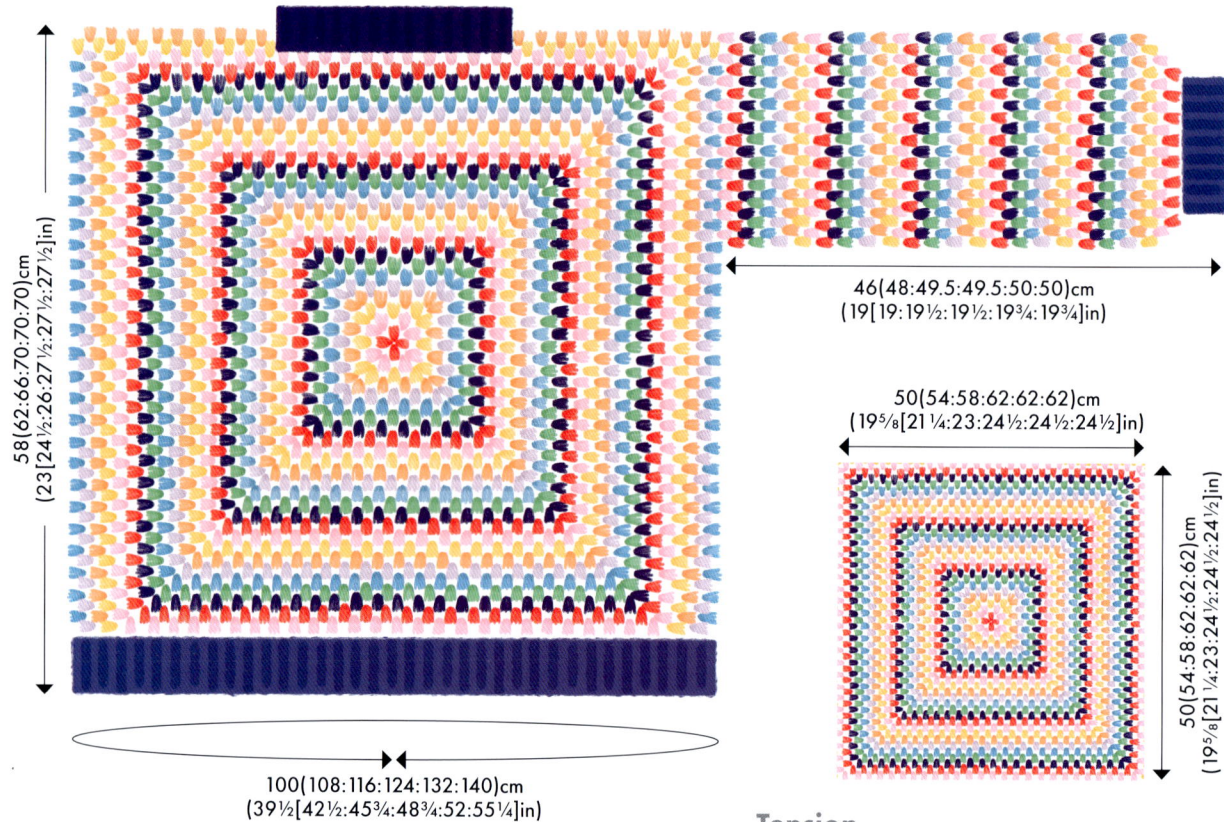

58(62:66:70:70:70)cm
(23[24½:26:27½:27½:27½]in)

46(48:49.5:49.5:50:50)cm
(19[19:19½:19½:19¾:19¾]in)

100(108:116:124:132:140)cm
(39½[42½:45¾:48¾:52:55¼]in)

50(54:58:62:62:62)cm
(19⅝[21¼:23:24½:24½:24½]in)

50(54:58:62:62:62)cm
(19⅝[21¼:23:24½:24½:24½]in)

Tension

- Large back granny square measures
  50(54:58:62:62:62) x 50(54:58:62:62:62)
  cm (19⅝[21¼:23:24½:24½:24½] x
  19⅝[21¼:23:24½:24½:24½] in) using size
  3.5mm (E/4) hook.

Large granny square

(make 2)

With yarn B, 4 ch, sl st to first ch to form a ring.

Round 1 (RS): 3 ch (counts as 1 tr here and throughout) 2 tr in ring, 2 ch, (3 tr, 2 ch) three times in ring, join with sl st to top of 3-ch, turn. Fasten off. Join yarn C in any corner 2-ch sp.

Round 2 (WS): 3 ch, (2 tr, 2 ch, 3 tr) in same 2 ch-sp, (3 tr, 2 ch, 3 tr) in each 2-ch sp, sl st to join, turn. Fasten off. Join yarn D in any corner 2-ch sp.

Round 3: 3 ch, (2 tr, 2 ch, 3 tr) in same 2-ch sp, 3 tr in sp between 3-tr groups, *(3 tr, 2 ch, 3 tr) in next 2-ch sp, 3 tr between 3-tr groups; rep from * twice more, sl st to top of 3-ch, turn. Fasten off. Join yarn E in any corner 2-ch sp.

Round 4: 3 ch, (2 tr, 2 ch, 3 tr) in same 2-ch sp, [3 tr in sp between 3-tr groups] twice, *(3 tr, 2 ch, 3 tr) in next 2-ch sp, [3 tr between 3-tr groups] twice; rep from * twice more, sl st to top of 3-ch, turn. Fasten off. Join yarn F in any corner 2-ch sp.

Round 5: 3 ch, (2 tr, 2 ch, 3 tr) in same 2-ch sp, 3 tr in sp between 3-tr groups to next corner, *(3 tr, 2 ch, 3 tr) in next 2-ch sp, 3 tr in sp between 3-tr groups to next corner; rep from * twice more, sl st to top of 3-ch, turn. Fasten off. Change to yarn G.

Round 6: as round 5.

Round 7: as round 5 using yarn H.

Round 8: as round 5 using yarn A.

Rounds 9–27(29:31:33:33): as round 5 keeping in colour sequence of one round in each of yarns B, C, D, E, F, G, H, A. Fasten off.

Widening rows

Sizes 5 and 6 only

Keeping colour sequence correct, join next yarn in any corner 2-ch sp.

Row 1 (WS): 3 ch (counts as 1 tr), 1 tr in same corner 2-ch sp, 3 tr in sp between 3-tr groups to next corner 2-ch sp, 1 tr in 2 ch-sp, 1 tr in last tr, turn. Fasten off. Join next yarn in top of last tr.

Row 2 (RS): 3 ch, 3 tr in sp between 3-tr groups to end, turn.

Size 6 only

Rep last 2 rows once more. Fasten off.

Repeat on opposite side of Granny Square.

The striped sleeves match the colours used for the squares, but you could easily change the look of the jumper by working the sleeves all in one colour.

Back neck

Take the first granny square and, keeping colour sequence correct throughout, cont as follows:

Sizes 1, 2, 3 and 4 only

Join next yarn shade in any corner 2 ch-sp.

Row 1: 3 ch (counts as first tr), 1 tr in same st, 3 tr in sp between 3-tr groups to end of row, 2 tr in last ch-sp, turn.

Size 5 only

Join next yarn shade under row end of last widening row.

Row 1: 3 ch, 1 tr under same row end, 3 tr under next row end, 3 tr in sp between 3-tr groups along, 3 tr under first row end, 2 tr under last row end, turn.

Size 6 only

Join next yarn shade under row end of last widening row.

Row 1: 3 ch, 1 tr under same row end, 3 tr under next row end, 1 tr under next row end, 2 tr under next row end (last 3 tr counts as one 3-tr group), 3 tr in sp between 3-tr groups to end, 1 tr under next row end, 2 tr under next row end (last 3 tr counts as one 3-tr group), 3 tr under next row end, 2 tr under last row end, turn.

All sizes

Row 2: 3 ch, 3 tr in sp between 3-tr groups, 1 tr in last tr, turn.

Row 3: 3 ch, 1 tr in same st, miss 3 tr, 3 tr in sp between 3-tr groups to last 4 tr, miss 3 tr, 2 tr in last tr, turn.

Row 4: as row 2.

Fasten off.

This garment can be made to suit any body shape or type. Go up a size if you want it to hang loosely and be the perfect baggy jumper.

Shape front shoulder

Take the second granny square and, keeping colour sequence correct throughout, cont as follows:

Sizes 1, 2, 3 and 4 only

Join next yarn shade in any corner 2-ch sp.

Row 1: 3 ch (counts as first tr), 1 tr in same st, 3 tr in next 9(10:10:11: -:-) sp between tr, 1 tr in next tr, turn.

Size 5 only

Join next yarn shade under row end of last widening row.

Row 1: 3 ch, 1 tr under same row end, 3 tr under next row end, 3 tr in next 11 sp between 3-tr groups, 1 tr in next tr, turn.

Size 6 only

Join next yarn shade under row end of last widening row.

Row 1: 3 ch, 1 tr under same row end, 3 tr under next row end, 1 tr under next row end, 2 tr under next row end (counts as one 3-tr group) 3 tr in next 11 sp between 3-tr groups, 1 tr in next tr, turn.

All sizes

Fasten off. Join next yarn in top of last tr.

Row 2: 3 ch, miss 3 tr, 3 tr in sp between 3-tr groups to end, 1 tr in last tr, turn.

Fasten off. Join next yarn in top of last tr.

Row 3: 3 ch, 1 tr in space between 1 tr and first 3-tr group, 3 tr in sp between 3-tr groups to last 4 tr, miss 3 tr, 1 tr in last tr, turn.

Fasten off. Join next yarn in top of last tr.

Row 4: as row 2.

Fasten off.

Second shoulder

Sizes 1, 2, 3 and 4 only

Join next yarn in 10th (11th:11th:12th:-:-) space in from opposite side, 3 ch, 3 tr in each of next 9 (10:10:11:-:-) spaces between 3-tr groups, 2 tr in corner ch-sp, turn.

Size 5 only

Join next yarn in 12th space in from opposite side, 3 ch, 3 tr in each of next 11 spaces between 3-tr groups, 3 tr under next row end, 2 tr under last row end, turn.

Size 6 only

Join next yarn in 12th space in from opposite side, 3 ch, 3 tr in each of next 11 spaces between 3-tr groups, 1 tr under next row end, 2 tr under next row end (counts as one 3-tr group), 3 tr under next row end, 2 tr under last row end, turn.

All sizes

Fasten off. Join next yarn in top of last tr.

Row 2: 3 ch, 3 tr in sp between 3-tr groups to last 4 tr, miss 3 tr, 1 tr in last tr, turn.

Fasten off. Join next yarn in top of last tr.

Row 3: 3 ch, miss 3 tr, 3 tr in sp between 3-tr groups to end, 1 tr in last tr, turn.

Fasten off. Join next yarn in top of last tr.

Row 4: as row 2.

Fasten off.

Sleeves

(make 2)

Cuff

Using yarn A, 12 ch.

Row 1: 1 dc in second ch from hook and in each ch to end, turn (11 sts).

Rows 2–33(33:33:36:36:39): 1 ch (does not count as a st), dc blo in each st to end, turn.

Sew together using a neat whip st along short edges.

Arm

Row 1: join yarn A in seam, work 1 dc in each row end, sl st to first dc to join, turn (33[33:33:36:36:39] sts).

Row 2: 1 ch (does not count as a st), 2 dc in each dc to end (66[66:66:72:72:78] sts).

Fasten off.

Working in colour sequence as for large granny square cont as follows:

Row 3: join yarn in any dc, 3 ch (counts as first tr), 2 tr in same st, miss 2 dc, [3 tr in next dc, miss 2 dc] around, sl st to top of 3-ch to join, turn.

Fasten off.

Rows 4–45(45:46:46:47:47): join next yarn in sp between any two 3-tr groups, 3 ch, 2 tr in same sp, 3 tr in sp between 3-tr groups around, sl st to top of 3-ch to join, turn. Fasten off.

Making up

Join at the shoulders using a neat whip stitch. Join at the sides leaving a gap for the armhole, and sew in the sleeves.

Opposite: To make the jumper uniform, the neck edging and cuffs are worked in the same colour (yarn A). However, you can choose any colour from the palette to create these sections.

Welt

Set-up round: join yarn A to a side seam at bottom edge, 1 ch (does not count as a st), work around entire bottom edge working 2 dc under each row end of widening rows on larger sizes and 1 dc in each tr, (do not work in ch sps), 12 ch, turn.

Row 1: 1 dc in second ch from hook and in each of next 11 ch, sl st in next dc of main round, sl st in foll dc, turn.

Row 2: tr blo to end, 1 ch, turn.

Row 3: tr blo to end, sl st in next st of main round, sl st in foll st, turn.

Rep rows 2 and 3 around entire bottom edge of garment.

Fasten off.

Neck edging

Set-up round: join yarn A to left seam at top edge, 1 ch (does not count as a st), work around entire neck edge working 2 dc under each row end of front shaping and 1 dc in each tr, (do not work in ch sps), 7 ch, turn.

Row 1: 1 dc in second ch from hook and in each of next 6 ch, sl st in next dc of main round, sl st in foll dc, turn.

Row 2: tr blo to end, 1 ch, turn.

Row 3: tr blo to end, sl st in next st of main round, sl st in foll st, turn.

Rep rows 2 and 3 around entire neck edge of garment, sl st short ends together.

Fasten off.

Weave in yarn ends.

Retro T-Shirt

This cute little T-shirt in its retro colour palette is sure to bring some 60s style to your wardrobe.

Tools and materials

Scheepjes Cotton 8, 100% cotton
50g (1¾oz) = 170m (186yd)

Yarn A: Ochre 722 x
2(2:2:3:3:3:3:4:4) balls

Yarn B: Rust 671 x
2(2:2:2:3:3:3:3:4:4) balls

Yarn C: Peach 649 x
2(2:2:3:3:3:3:4:4) balls

Yarn D: Bright Blue 563 x
2(2:2:2:3:3:3:4:4) balls

Yarn E: Navy 527 x
2(2:2:2:3:3:3:4:4) balls

Yarn F: Grey Blue 652 x
1(1:2:2:3:3:3:4:4) balls

Yarn G: Light Grey 700 x
1(1:2:2:3:3:3:4:4) balls

Size 3.5mm (E/4) hook

Yarn needle

Yarn substitutes

Any 4-ply weight yarn that works to the same tension would be a suitable substitute.

See also

• The classic granny square, page 14

This T-shirt combines joined granny squares with rows of granny stitches to create a unique and fun look.

Sizes and schematic

To fit	1	2	3	4	5	6	7	8	9	
Actual chest approx	88	96	104	112	120	128	136	144	152	cm
	34⅝	37¾	41	44	46¾	50⅜	53½	56¾	60	in
Length approx	47	51	55	59	63	63	63	63	63	cm
	18½	20	21¾	23¼	24¾	24¾	24¾	24¾	24¾	in
Sleeve seam approx	9	10	10	11	11	11	12	12	12	cm
	3½	4	4	4⅜	4⅜	4⅜	4¾	4¾	4¾	in

47(51:55:59:63:63:63:63:63)cm
(18½[20:21¾:23¼:24¾:24¾:24¾:24¾:24¾]in)

9(10:10:11:11:11:12:12:12)cm
(3½[4:4:4⅜:4⅜:4⅜:4¾:4¾:4¾]in)

88(96:104:112:120:128:136:144:152)cm
(34⅝[37¾:41:44:46¾:50⅜:53½:56¾:60]in)

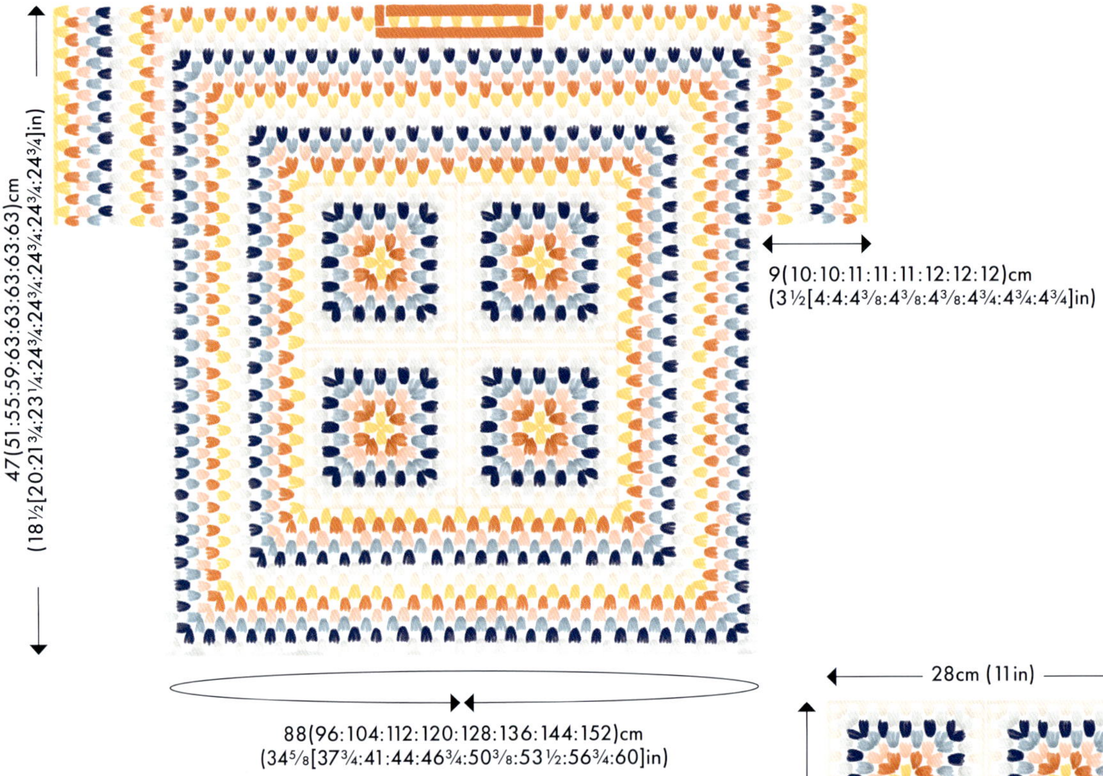

Tension

- Small granny square measures 14 x 14cm (5½ x 5½in) using size 3.5mm (E/4) hook.
- 18 sts x 10 rows in patt to 10 x 10cm (4 x 4in).

14cm (5½in)

14cm (5½in)

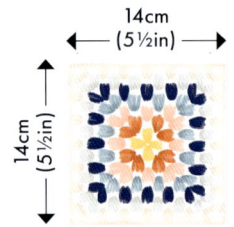

28cm (11in)

28cm (11in)

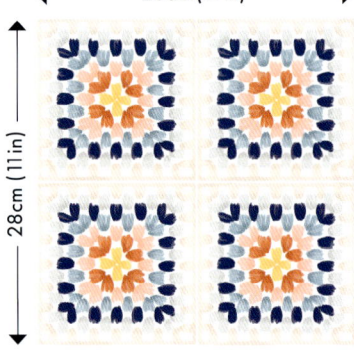

Join four motifs together

Granny square

(make eight)

Turn at end of each round.

With yarn A, 4 ch, sl st to first ch to form ring.

Round 1 (RS): 3 ch (counts as 1 tr here and throughout) 2 tr in ring, 2 ch, (3 tr, 2 ch) three times in ring, join with sl st to top of 3-ch, turn. Fasten off. Join yarn B in any 2-ch sp.

Round 2 (WS): 3 ch, (2 tr, 2 ch, 3 tr) in same 2-ch sp, (3 tr, 2 ch, 3 tr) in each 2-ch sp, sl st to join, turn. Fasten off. Join yarn C in any corner 2-ch sp.

Round 3: 3 ch, (2 tr, 2 ch, 3 tr) in corner 2-ch sp, 3 tr in space between each 3-tr group to next corner 2-ch sp, *(3 tr, 2 ch, 3 tr) in corner 2-ch sp, 3 tr in space between each 3-tr group to next corner 2-ch sp; rep from * twice more, sl st to join, turn. Fasten off. Join yarn D in any corner 2-ch sp.

Round 4: 3 ch, (2 tr, 2 ch, 3 tr) in corner 2-ch sp, 3 tr in space between each 3-tr group to next corner 2-ch sp, *(3 tr, 2 ch, 3 tr) in corner 2-ch sp, 3 tr in space between each 3-tr group to next corner 2-ch sp; rep from * twice more, sl st to join, turn. Fasten off. Join yarn E in any corner 2-ch sp.

Round 5: as round 4. Fasten off. Join yarn F in any corner 2-ch sp.

Round 6: as round 5. Fasten off. Join yarn G in any corner 2-ch sp.

Round 7: as round 5. Fasten off.

Joining

Join on round 7 using the continual joining method (see page 136) or use a neat whip stitch and follow the layout shown on the schematic.

The T-shirt is shaped around the neck and shoulders for a comfortable fit and a stylish, neat finish.

The four squares on the back panel are the same as the ones on the front. Change the colour order on the back if you want to easily distinguish the back from the front.

Back

Join yarn A in any corner 2-ch sp.

Round 1: 3 ch (counts as 1 tr), (2 tr, 2 ch, 3 tr) in same corner sp, 3 tr in space between each 3-tr group to corner space of first square, miss this corner space, work 3 tr in join between both squares, miss first corner space of second square, 3 tr in space between each 3-tr group to next corner of second square, *(3 tr, 2 ch, 3 tr) in corner 2-ch sp, 3 tr in space between each 3-tr group to join between squares, miss corner ch-sp, 3 tr in join between squares, miss next corner ch-sp, 3 tr in space between each 3-tr group to second corner ch-sp of square; rep from * twice more around remaining sides of square, sl st to top of beg 3-ch to join, turn.

Fasten off. Join yarn B in any corner 2-ch sp.

Round 2: 3 ch, (2 tr, 2 ch, 3 tr) in corner 2-ch sp, 3 tr in space between each 3-tr group to next corner 2-ch sp, *(3 tr, 2 ch, 3 tr) in corner 2-ch sp, 3 tr in space between each 3-tr group to next corner 2-ch sp; rep from * twice more, sl st to join, turn.

Fasten off.

Rounds 3–8 (10:12:14:16:16:16:16:16): work as round 2, continuing to work in colour sequence of A, B, C, D, E, F, G and starting round 3 with C.**

Widening rows

Sizes 6, 7, 8 and 9 only

Fastening off at the end of each row and, keeping colour sequence correct, cont as follows:

Join next yarn shade in any corner 2-ch sp.

Row 1: 3 ch, 3 tr in same 2-ch space, 3 tr between each 3-tr group to end of row, 4 tr in corner ch-sp, turn.

Fasten off. Join next yarn shade in top of last tr.

Row 2: 3 ch, 1 tr in same st, 3 tr in space between each 3-tr group to end of row, 2 tr in top of last st, turn.

Fasten off. Join next yarn shade in top of last tr.

Sizes 7, 8 and 9 only

Row 3: 3 ch, 3 tr in space before each 3-tr group to end, 1 tr in last tr, turn.

Row 4: rep row 2.
Size 7 fasten off.

Size 8 only

Rep last 2 rows once more.
Fasten off.

Size 9 only

Rep last 2 rows twice more.
Fasten off. ✱✱✱

Shape top back of neck

Sizes 1, 2, 3, 4 and 5 only

Keeping colour sequence correct, join next yarn in any corner 2-ch sp.

Row 1: 3 ch, 1 tr in same sp, 3 tr in space between each 3-tr group to first corner 2-ch sp, 2 tr in corner 2-ch sp, turn.

Fasten off. Join next yarn shade in top of last tr.

Sizes 6, 7, 8 and 9 only

Keeping colour sequence correct, join next yarn in under last row end of widening row.

Row 1: 3 ch, 1 tr under same row end, [miss next row end, 3 tr under next row end] -(-:-:-:-:1:2:3:4) times, 3 tr in space between each 3-tr group to last corner 2-ch sp of main granny square, 3 tr in corner 2-ch sp, [miss next row end, 3 tr under next row end] -(-:-:-:-:0:1:2:3) times, miss next row end, 2 tr under last row end, turn.

Fasten off. Join next yarn shade in top of last tr.

All sizes

Row 2: 3 ch, 3 tr in space between each 3-tr group to end, 1 tr in top of 3-ch, turn.

Fasten off, join next yarn shade in top of last tr.

Row 3: 3 ch, 1 tr in space before first 3-tr group, 3 tr in space between each 3-tr group to end, 1 tr in space before last st, 1 tr in last st.

Fasten off.

Front

Sizes 1, 2, 3, 4 and 5 only

Work as for Back to ✱✱.

Shape left shoulder

Keeping colour sequence correct, join next yarn in any corner 2-ch sp.
Row 1: 3 ch, 1 tr in same sp, 3 tr in next 7(8:9:9:10) spaces between 3-tr groups, 1 tr in next space, turn.
Fasten off, join next yarn shade in top of last tr.
Row 2: 3 ch, miss 3 tr, 3 tr in next 7(8:9:9:10) spaces between 3-tr groups, 1 tr in last tr, turn.
Fasten off, join next yarn shade in top of last tr.

Row 3: 3 ch, 1 tr in space before first 3-tr group, 3 tr in each of next 7(8:9:9:10) spaces between 3-tr groups, 1 tr in last tr.
Fasten off.

Shape right shoulder

Join yarn in 8(9:10:10:11)th space along from outside edge,
3 ch, 3 tr in each space between 3-tr groups to corner, 2 tr in corner space, turn.
Fasten off, join next yarn shade in top of last tr.
Row 2: 3 ch, 3 tr in space before first 3-tr group and in each of next in next 7(8:9:9:10) spaces, miss 3 tr, 1 tr in last tr, turn.
Fasten off, join next yarn shade in top of last tr.
Row 3: 3 ch, 3 tr in each of next in next 7(8:9:9:10) spaces between 3-tr groups, 1 tr in space before last tr, 1 tr in last tr.
Fasten off.

Sizes 6, 7, 8 and 9 only
Work as for Back to ***.

Shape left shoulder (2)

Keeping colour sequence correct, join next yarn under last row end.
Row 1: 3 ch, 1 tr under same row end, miss next row end, [3 tr under next row end, miss next row end] -(-:-:-:-:0:1:2:3) times, 3 tr in corner 2-ch sp of main granny square, 3 tr in next 9 spaces between 3-tr groups, 1 tr in next space, turn.
Fasten off, join next yarn shade in top of last tr.
Row 2: 3 ch, miss 3 tr, 3 tr in space between each 3-tr group to end, 1 tr in last tr, turn.
Fasten off, join next yarn shade in top of last tr.
Row 3: 3 ch, 1 tr in space before first 3-tr group, 3 tr between 3-tr group, to end 1 tr in last tr.
Fasten off.

Shape right shoulder (2)

Join yarn in 10th space along from outside edge, 3 ch, 3 tr in each space between 3-tr group along main granny square working 3 tr in corner 2-ch sp, miss next row end, [3 tr under next row end, miss next row end] -(-, -:-:-:0:1:2:3) times, 2 tr under last row end, turn.
Fasten off, join next yarn shade in top of last tr.
Row 2: 3 ch, 3 tr in space before first 3-tr group to end, 1 tr in last tr, turn.
Fasten off, join next yarn shade in top of last tr.
Row 3: 3 ch, 3 tr between each 3-tr group to end, 1 tr in space before last tr, 1 tr in last tr.
Fasten off.

Sleeves

Work both sleeves in the same way.

Working in colour sequence as set and beg with yarn A, work 52 (64:73:82:91:97:103:109:109) ch.

Row 1: 1 tr in fourth ch from hook (missed 3 ch counts as 1 tr), [miss 2 ch, 3 tr in next ch] to last 3 ch, miss 2 ch, 2 tr in last ch, turn.

Fasten off, join next yarn shade in top of last tr.

Row 2: 3 ch, 3 tr in each space between 3-tr groups to end, 1 tr in last st, turn.

Fasten off, join next yarn shade in top of last tr.

Row 3: 3 ch, 1 tr before first 3-tr group, 3 tr in each space between 3-tr groups to end, 1 tr in space before last st, 1 tr in last top of 3-ch, turn.

Fasten off, join next yarn shade in top of last tr.

Rows 4–9 (10:10:11:11:11:12:12:12): rep rows 2 and 3 keeping in colour sequence.

Fasten off.

Finishing

Using a neat whip stitch, sew the front to the back at the shoulder. Fold the sleeves in half and, matching this point to the shoulder seam, sew the sleeves in place. Sew side and sleeve seams.

Neck

Using your yarn shade of choice, join in yarn in the side seam of the neck.

Round 1: 1 ch (does not count as a st) work 1 dc in each st and 2 dc in each row end around entire neck opening, sl st to join.

Fasten off.

Experiment with making the sleeves longer or shorter for different looks and different seasons.

Weave in yarn ends.

Cozy Cropped Cardigan

This gorgeous, cozy cropped cardigan is perfect for popping on over a summer dress or for keeping off the chill on evening walks along the pier or the seafront.

Tools and materials

Scheepjes Softfun DK, 60% cotton, 40% acrylic
50g (1¾oz) = 140m (153yd)
Yarn A: Orchid 2657 x 6(7:8:9:11:12) balls
Yarn B: Cantaloupe 2652 x 1 ball
Yarn C: Coral 2607 x 1 ball

Yarn D: Purple 2463 x 2 balls
Yarn E: Hot Pink 2495 1 x 2 ball
Yarn F: Lace 2426 x 3 balls
Size 4.5mm (7) hook
Yarn needle

Yarn substitutes

Any DK weight yarn that works to the same tension would be a suitable substitute.

See also

• The classic granny square, page 14

Accentuate the cropped cardigan with a tucked-in top and a pair of high-waisted trousers.

Sizes and schematic

This garment is designed to be worn loose and roomy. Choose the size nearest to your actual chest size for a less oversized fit.

Size	1	2	3	4	5	6	
Actual chest	112	120	128	136	144	152	cm
	44	47¼	50½	53½	56¾	60	in
Length	45	48	51	54	57	57	cm
	17¾	19	20	21¼	22½	22½	in
Sleeve length	44	44	39.5	39.5	39.5	39.5	cm
	17¼	17¼	15½	15½	15½	15½	in

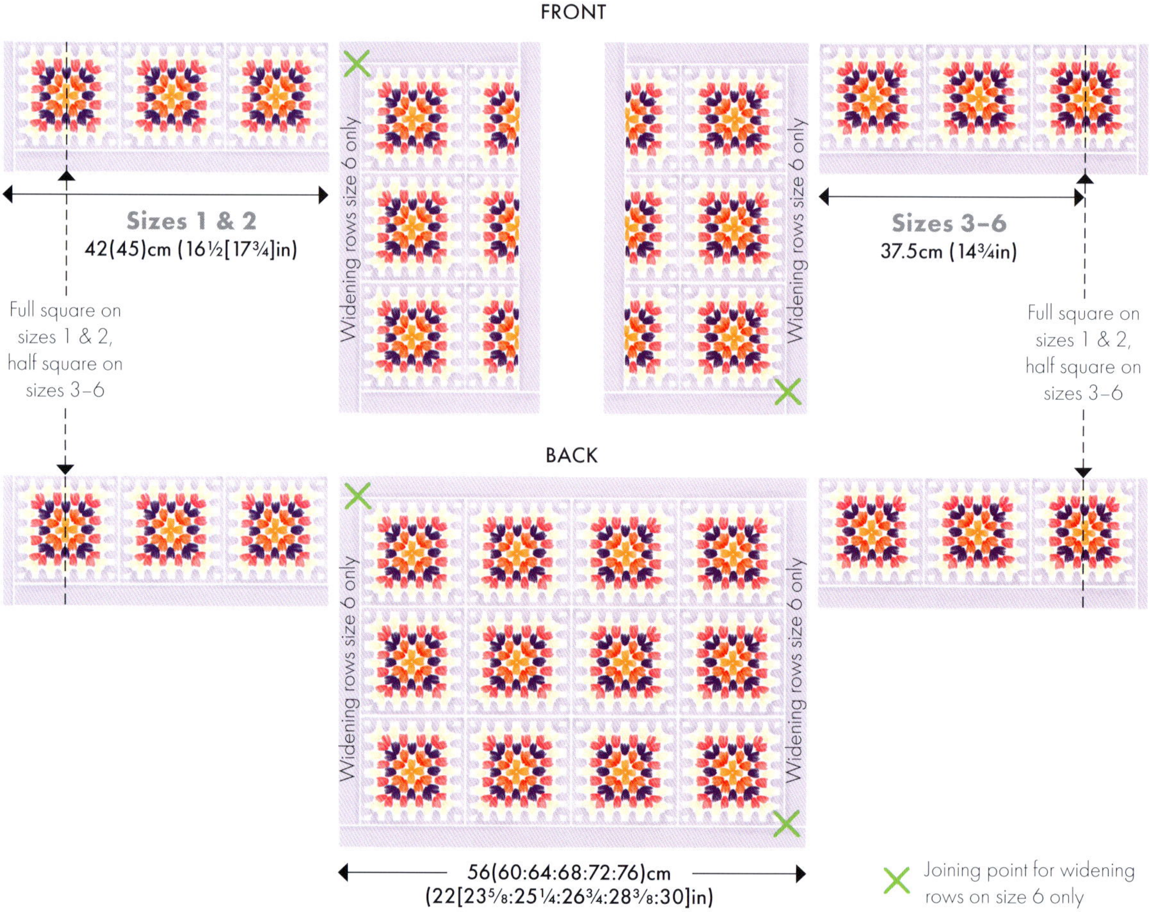

FRONT

Widening rows size 6 only

Sizes 1 & 2
42(45)cm (16½[17¾]in)

Full square on sizes 1 & 2, half square on sizes 3–6

Sizes 3–6
37.5cm (14¾in)

Full square on sizes 1 & 2, half square on sizes 3–6

BACK

Widening rows size 6 only

56(60:64:68:72:76)cm
(22[23⅝:25¼:26¾:28⅜:30]in)

✕ Joining point for widening rows on size 6 only

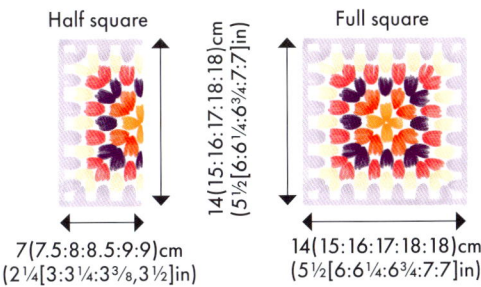

Half square

14(15:16:17:18:18]cm
(5½[6:6¼:6¾:7:7]in)

7(7.5:8:8.5:9:9)cm
(2¼[3:3¼:3⅜,3½]in)

Full square

14(15:16:17:18:18)cm
(5½[6:6¼:6¾:7:7]in)

Tension

- Each square measures 14(15:16:17:18:18)
  x 14(15:16:17:18:18)cm (5½[6:6¼:6¾:7:7]
  x 5½[6:6¼:6¾:7:7]in) using a size 4.5mm
  (7) hook or size required to obtain correct
  tension.

Full square

Sizes 1 and 2 only
Make 30 full squares and 6 half squares as given for size.

Sizes 3, 4, 5 and 6 only
Body: make 18 full squares and 6 half squares as given for size.
Sleeves: make 8 full squares in size 2 to end of round 7 and 4 half squares in size 2 to end of row 7.

Using yarn B, 4 ch, sl st to first ch to form ring.
Round 1 (RS): 3 ch (counts as tr here and throughout) 2 tr in ring, 2 ch, (3 tr, 2 ch) three times in ring, join with sl st to top of 3-ch, turn.
Fasten off yarn B. Join yarn C in any 2-ch sp.
Round 2 (WS): 3 ch, (2 tr, 2 ch, 3 tr) in same 2-ch sp, (3 tr, 2 ch, 3 tr) in each of next three 2-ch sps, sl st to join, turn.
Fasten off yarn C. Join yarn D in any 2-ch sp.

Round 3 (RS): 3 ch, (2 tr, 2 ch, 3 tr) in same 2-ch sp, 3 tr in space before next 3-tr group, *(3 tr, 2 ch, 3 tr) in next 2-ch sp, 3 tr in space before next 3-tr group; rep from * twice more, sl st to top of beg 3-ch, turn.
Fasten off yarn D. Join yarn E in any 2-ch sp.
Round 4 (WS): 3 ch, (2 tr, 2 ch, 3 tr) in same 2-ch sp, 3 tr in space before each 3-tr group to corner 2-ch sp, *(3 tr, 2 ch, 3 tr) in next 2-ch sp, 3 tr in space before each 3-tr group to next corner 2-ch sp; rep from * twice more, sl st to top of beg 3-ch, turn.
Fasten off yarn E. Join yarn F in any 2-ch sp.
Round 5 (RS): as round 4.
Fasten off yarn F. Join yarn A in any 2-ch sp.
Round 6 (WS): as round 4.

Size 2 only
Round 7 (RS): * 1 dc in tr to next corner 2-ch sp, (1 dc, 2 ch, 1 dc) in 2-ch sp; rep from * around, sl st to first dc to join.

Sizes 3, 4, 5 and 6 only
Round 7 (RS): sl st to first sp between tr, 3 ch, 2 tr in same space, 3 tr in space between each 3-tr group and (3 tr, 2 ch, 3 tr) in each corner 2-ch sp around, sl st to top of beg 3-ch.

Size 4 only
Round 8 (WS): 1 dc in tr to next corner 2-ch sp, (1 dc, 2 ch, 1 dc) in 2-ch sp; rep from * around, sl st to first dc to join.

Sizes 5 and 6 ONLY
Round 8 (WS): rep round 7.

Fasten off ALL SIZES.

Half square

Using yarn B, 4 ch, sl st to first ch to form ring.

Row 1 (RS): 3 ch (counts as first tr here and throughout), (1 tr, 2 ch, 2 tr) in ring, turn.

Fasten off yarn B. Join yarn C in top of last st.

Row 2 (WS): 3 ch, (3 tr, 2 ch, 3 tr) in each of next two 2-ch sps, 1 tr in last tr, turn.

Fasten off yarn C. Join yarn D in top of last st.

Row 3 (RS): 3 ch, 1 tr in space before next 3-tr group, (3 tr, 2 ch, 3 tr) in 2-ch sp, 3 tr in space before next 3-tr group, (3 tr, 2 ch, 3 tr) in 2-ch sp, 1 tr before last tr, 1 tr in last st, turn.

Fasten off yarn D. Join yarn E in top of last st.

Row 4 (WS): 3 ch, 3 tr in space before next 3-tr group, (3 tr, 2 ch, 3 tr) in corner 2-ch sp, 3 tr in space between next two 3-tr groups, (3 tr, 2 ch, 3 tr) in corner 2-ch sp, 3 tr in space before last 2 tr, 1 tr in last tr, turn.

Fasten off yarn E. Join yarn F in top of last st.

Row 5 (RS): 3 ch, 1 tr in space before next 3-tr group, 3 tr in space before next 3-tr group, (3 tr, 2 ch, 3 tr) in corner 2-ch sp, 3 tr in space before each 3-tr group to next corner, (3 tr, 2 ch, 3 tr) in corner 2-ch sp, 3 tr in space before next 3-tr group, 1 tr in space before last tr, 1 tr in last tr, turn.

Fasten off yarn F. Join yarn A in top of last st.

Row 6 (WS): 3 ch, *3 tr in space before each 3-tr group to corner 2-ch sp, (3 tr, 2 ch, 3 tr) in corner 2-ch sp; rep from * once more, 3 tr in space before each 3 tr to last 2 tr, 1 tr in last st, turn.

Size 2 only

Row 7 (RS): 1 dc in each tr and (1 dc, 2 ch, 1 dc) in each 2-ch sp around, turn.

Sizes 3, 4, 5 and 6 only

Row 7 (RS): 3 ch, 1 tr in space before next 3-tr group, 3 tr in space before each 3-tr group to next corner, (3 tr, 2 ch, 3 tr) in corner 2-ch sp, 3 tr in space before each 3-tr group to next corner, (3 tr, 2 ch, 3 tr) in corner 2-ch sp, 3 tr in space before each 3-tr group to last tr, 1 tr in space before last tr, 1 tr in last tr, turn.

Size 4 only

Row 8 (WS): 1 dc in each tr and (1 dc, 2 ch, 1 dc) in each 2-ch sp around, turn.

Sizes 5 and 6 only

Row 8 (WS): rep row 6.

Fasten off ALL SIZES.

To join

Join squares as shown on schematic using a neat whip stitch.

Widening rows

Size 6 only

Rejoin yarn A in corner ch sp. Corner ch sp is indicated on the schematic with a green cross.

Row 1: 3 ch (counts as first tr), 1 tr in each st to end of row (do not work in ch sps between squares), 1 tr in 2-ch sp in corner ch sp at end of row, turn.

Row 2: 3 ch, tr to end.

Fasten off.

Repeat on the opposite side of the back and on both fronts, joining in the yarn at the centre of the green cross on each piece.

Finishing

Use yarn A throughout to finish as follows.

Back neck

Sizes 1 to 5 only

With RS facing, rejoin yarn A in top right corner ch-sp of back section.
Row 1 (RS): 3 ch (counts as 1 tr), 1 tr in each tr along, 1 tr in last corner ch sp, turn.
Row 2: 3 ch, tr to end.
Fasten off.

Size 6 only

With RS facing, rejoin yarn A in top right corner of back section under tr row end of widening row.
Row 1 (RS): 3 ch (counts as 1 tr), 1 tr under same row end, 2 tr under next row end, 1 tr in each tr along, 2 tr under each of next two tr row ends, turn.
Row 2: 3 ch, tr to end.
Fasten off.

Front neck

Worked in the same way on both sides of the front.

Sizes 1 to 5 only

With RS facing, rejoin yarn A in top right corner ch sp of front section.
Row 1 (RS): 3 ch (counts as 1 tr), 1 tr in each tr along, 1 tr in last corner ch sp, turn.
Row 2: 3 ch, tr to end.
Fasten off.
Repeat for the second side of the front.

Size 6 only

First side: with RS facing rejoin yarn A in top right corner of front section under tr row end of widening row.
Row 1 (RS): 3 ch (counts as 1 tr), 1 tr in same row end, 2 tr under next row end, 1 tr in each tr along, turn.
Row 2: 3 ch, tr to end.
Fasten off.
Second side: with RS facing rejoin yarn A in top right corner ch sp of front section.
Row 1 (RS): 3 ch (counts as 1 tr), 1 tr in each tr to end, working 2 tr under each of two widening row ends, turn.
Row 2: 3 ch, tr to end.
Fasten off.

Experiment with different yarns that work to the same tension for a warmer or cooler cardigan.

The low-hanging sleeves add to the cozy aesthetic of this piece. However, if you prefer pushed up sleeves, a flexible hair tie placed over the sleeve and below the elbow is a great hack for holding the fabric in place.

Front edging

Worked in the same way on both sides of the front.

With RS facing, rejoin yarn A under first row end of half square at front edge.

Row 1: 3 ch (counts as 1 tr), work 2 dc under each tr row end, 1 dc under each dc row end and 1 dc into centre 4 ch of each half square all along, turn.

Row 2: 1 ch, dc to end.

Fasten off.

Repeat for second front.

Now sew fronts to back at shoulder using a neat whip stitch and matching stitch for stitch along.

Make up sleeves

Join sleeve squares together as shown on schematic to make four strips, with three full squares for sizes 1 and 2 and two full squares and one half square for sizes 3–6.

With RS facing, rejoin yarn A in corner ch sp of one long edge.

Row 1: 3 ch (counts as first tr), work 1 tr in each tr along all squares to end, turn.

Row 2: 3 ch, tr to end, turn.

Fasten off.

Repeat these 2 rows along the bottom long edge of each sleeve section.

Using a neat whip stitch, join two strips together along the top edge of the squares, making sure that tr rows are at the bottom edge so that they sit at the underarm position. Fold each sleeve into a tube and sew together along the tr sts of the extra rows.

Cuff

Worked in the same way on both sleeves.

With RS facing, rejoin yarn A where extra rows are joined (on sizes 3–6 ensure you join at the half square end of the tube).

Round 1: 1 ch, work 1 dc in each st, 2 dc under each tr row end and 1 dc in centre 4 ch of each square along.

Fasten off.

Repeat on second sleeve.

Joining sleeves

Join the sleeves to the body, ensuring the extra tr rows are positioned under the arm. Also make sure to match the seam between squares at the top edge to the shoulder seam of the front and back.

Now join the side seams.

Bottom edging

With RS of garment facing, hold work upside down and rejoin yarn A to the bottom corner of the left front.

Row 1: 1 ch, work 1 dc in each st and 2 dc under each row end all around to bottom corner of right front, turn.

Row 2: 1 ch, dc to end, turn.

Row 3: 1 ch, dc to end, and continue in dc around entire front opening of garment ending back at the corner of the right front.

Fasten off.

Weave in all yarn ends.

Boho-Chic Maxi Waistcoat

This full-length, sweeping waistcoat will make you feel like a true free spirit. The unconventional and flowy style is perfect for channelling your inner wild child.

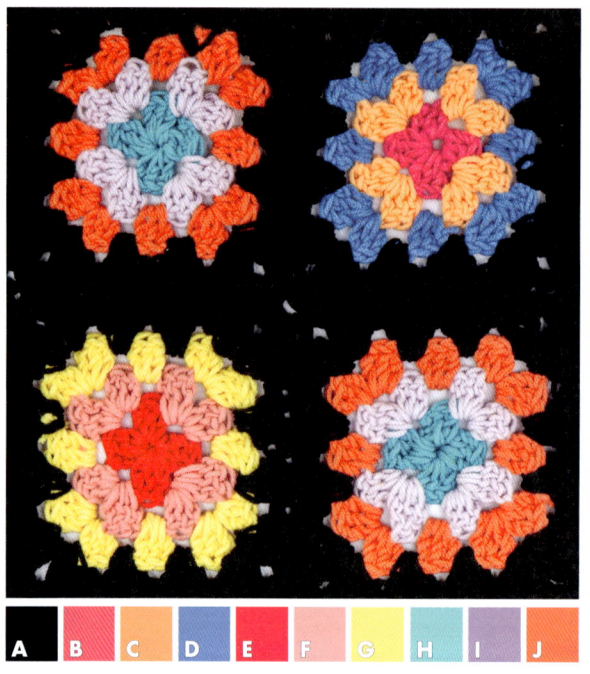

Tools and materials

Scheepjes Softfun DK, 60% cotton, 40% acrylic
50g (1¾oz) = 140m (153yd)

Yarn A: Black 2408 x 8(9:10:12:14:17) balls
Yarn B: Hot Pink 2495 x 1 ball
Yarn C: Cantaloupe 2652 x 1 ball
Yarn D: Azure 2629 x 2 balls
Yarn E: Magenta 2654 x 1 ball
Yarn F: Pink 2480 x 1 ball
Yarn G: Canary 2518 x 2 balls
Yarn H: Bright Turquoise 2423 x 1 ball
Yarn I: Violet 2519 x 1 ball
Yarn J: Salmon 2449 x 2 balls
Size 4.5mm (7) hook
Yarn needle

Yarn substitutes

Any DK weight yarn that works to the same tension would be a suitable substitute.

See also

• The classic granny square, page 14

This could be the perfect stash-buster if you have a lot of different colours on hand. Just purchase the correct number of balls for your base colour (in this case, black), and get hooking!

Schematic

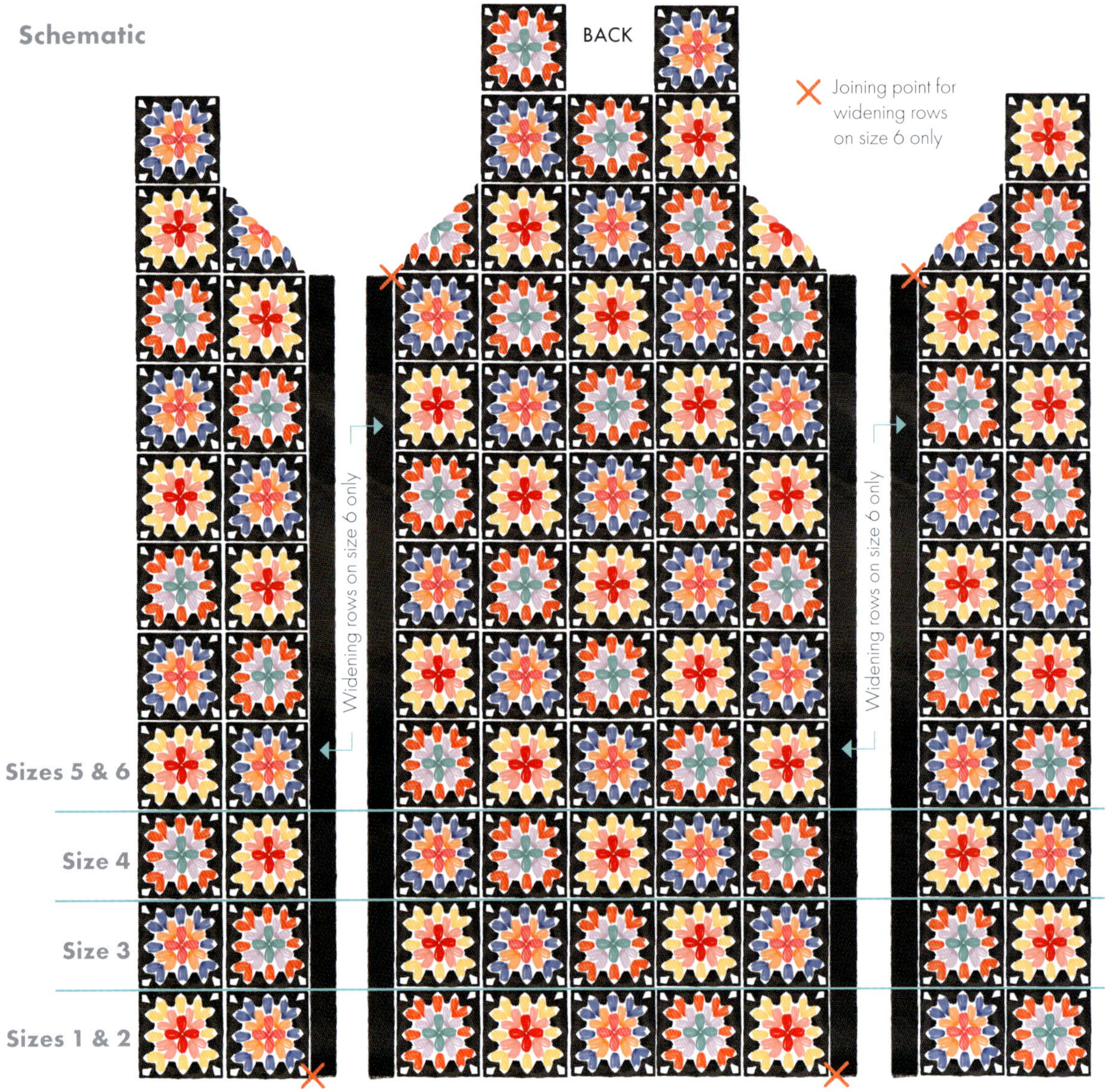
BACK
Joining point for widening rows on size 6 only
Widening rows on size 6 only
Widening rows on size 6 only
Sizes 5 & 6
Size 4
Size 3
Sizes 1 & 2

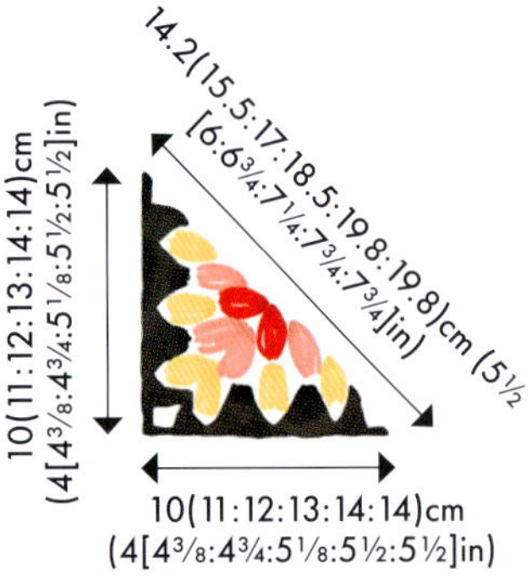
14.2(15.5:17:18.5:19.8:19.8)cm (5½ [6:6¾:7¼:7¾:7¾]in)
10(11:12:13:14:14)cm (4[4⅜:4¾:5⅛:5½:5½]in)
10(11:12:13:14:14)cm (4[4⅜:4¾:5⅛:5½:5½]in)

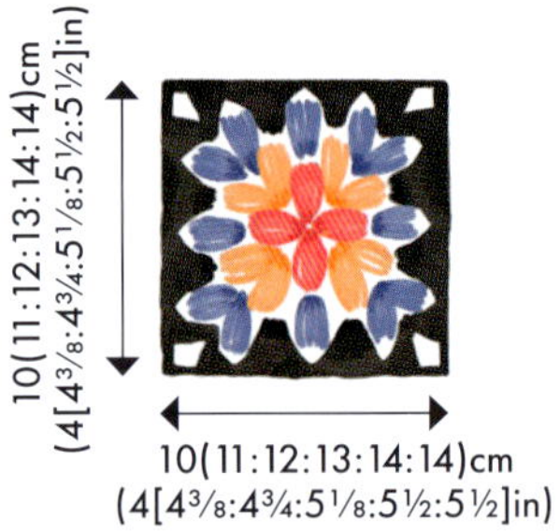
10(11:12:13:14:14)cm (4[4⅜:4¾:5⅛:5½:5½]in)
10(11:12:13:14:14)cm (4[4⅜:4¾:5⅛:5½:5½]in)

Tension

- Each square measures 10(11:12:13:14:14) x 10(11:12:13:14:14)cm (4[4⅜:4¾:5⅛:5½:5½] x 4[4⅜:4¾:5⅛:5½:5½]in) using size 4.5mm (7) hook or size required to obtain tension.

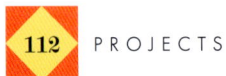

Sizes

	1	2	3	4	5	6	
Finished chest size	100	110	120	130	140	152	cm
	39⅜	43¼	47¼	51¼	55⅛	60	in
Finished length	117	117	128	125	124	124	cm
	46	46	50½	49¼	48¾	48¾	in

Full square

Square 1  **Square 2**   **Square 3**

Square 1
Round 1: yarn B.
Round 2: yarn C.
Round 3: yarn D.
Round 4: yarn A.

Square 2
Round 1: yarn E.
Round 2: yarn F.
Round 3: yarn G.
Round 4: yarn A.

Square 3
Round 1: yarn H.
Round 2: yarn I.
Round 3: yarn J.
Round 4: yarn A.

Using suggested yarn, 4 ch, sl st to first ch to form ring.
Round 1 (RS): 3 ch (counts as tr here and throughout) 2 tr in ring, 2 ch, (3 tr, 2 ch) three times in ring, join with sl st to top of 3-ch, turn.
Fasten off. Join next yarn in any 2-ch sp.
Round 2 (WS): 3 ch, (2 tr, 2 ch, 3 tr) in same 2-ch sp, (3 tr, 2 ch, 3 tr) in each of next three 2-ch sps, sl st to join, turn.
Fasten off. Join next yarn in any 2-ch sp.
Round 3 (RS): 3 ch, (2 tr, 2 ch, 3 tr) in same 2-ch sp, 3 tr in space before next 3-tr group, *(3 tr, 2 ch, 3 tr) in next 2-ch sp, 3 tr in space before next 3-tr group; rep from * twice more, sl st to top of beg 3-ch, turn.
Fasten off. Join yarn A in any 2-ch sp.
Round 4 (WS): 3 ch, (2 tr, 2 ch, 3 tr) in same 2-ch sp, 3 tr in space between each 3-tr group to corner 2-ch sp, *(3 tr, 2 ch, 3 tr) in next 2-ch sp, 3 tr in space between each 3-tr group to next corner 2-ch sp; rep from * twice more, sl st to top of beg 3-ch, turn.
Cont in yarn A only.

Size 2 only
Round 5 (RS): *1 dc in each tr to next corner 2-ch sp, (1 dc, 2 ch, 1 dc) in 2-ch sp; rep from * around, sl st to first dc to join.

Sizes 3, 4, 5 and 6 only
Round 5 (RS): sl st to first sp between tr, 3 ch, 2 tr in same space, 3 tr in space between each 3-tr group and (3 tr, 2 ch, 3 tr) in each corner 2-ch sp around, sl st to top of beg 3-ch.

Size 4 only
Round 6 (WS): *1 dc in each tr to next corner 2-ch sp, (1 dc, 2 ch, 1 dc) in 2-ch sp; rep from * around, sl st to first dc to join.

Sizes 5 and 6 only
Round 6 (RS): rep round 5.

Fasten off ALL SIZES.

Half diagonal granny square

Square 1

Square 2

Square 3

With suggested yarn, 4 ch, sl st to first ch to form ring.

Row 1 (RS): 4 ch (counts as 1 tr, 1 ch here and throughout), (3 tr, 2 ch, 3 tr, 1 ch, 1 tr) in ring, turn. Fasten off. Join next yarn in top of last tr.

Row 2 (WS): 4 ch, 3 tr in 1 ch-sp, (3 tr, 2 ch, 3 tr) in corner 2-ch sp, 3 tr in 1 ch-sp, 1 ch, 1 tr in third of 4-ch, turn.
Fasten off. Join next yarn in top of last tr.

Row 3 (RS): 4 ch, 3 tr in 1 ch-sp, 3 tr in space between 3-tr groups, (3 tr, 2 ch, 3 tr) in corner 2-ch sp, 3 tr in space between 3-tr groups, 3 tr in 1 ch-sp, 1 ch, 1 tr in third of 4-ch, turn.
Fasten off. Join yarn A in top of last dc.

Row 4 (WS): 4 ch, 3 tr in 1 ch-sp, 3 tr in space between each 3-tr group to corner 2-ch sp, (3 tr, 2 ch, 3 tr) in corner 2-ch sp, 3 tr in space between each 3-tr group to 1 ch-sp, 3 tr in 1 ch-sp, 1 ch, 1 tr in third of 4-ch, turn.

Size 2 only

Row 5 (RS): 1 dc in 1 ch-sp, 1 dc in each tr to corner 2-ch sp, (1 dc, 2 ch, 1 dc) in corner 2-ch sp, 1 dc in each tr to end, 1 dc in 1 ch-sp. Fasten off.

Sizes 3, 4, 5 and 6 only
Row 5 (RS): rep row 4.

Size 4 only
Row 6 (WS): 1 dc in 1 ch-sp, 1 dc in each tr to corner 2-ch sp, (1 dc, 2 ch, 1 dc) in corner 2-ch sp, 1 dc in each tr to end, 1 dc in 1 ch-sp.

Sizes 5 and 6 only
Row 6: rep row 4.

Fasten off ALL SIZES.

Make the following number of squares and corners in the three different colourways. Note the half squares need additional rows for increasing sizes. Check pattern text to determine how many rows are required:

Size	1	2	3	4	5	6
Full squares: Square 1	31	31	28	25	22	22
Full squares: Square 2	31	31	28	25	22	22
Full squares: Square 3	31	31	28	25	22	22
Half squares: Square 1	2	2	2	2	2	2
Half squares: Square 2	1	1	1	1	1	1
Half squares: Square 3	1	1	1	1	1	1

Reduce the number of squares if you prefer a shorter garment or need to adjust for your height. This model is 170cm (5'7") and it reaches her ankles.

Joining

Join squares for the front and back as shown on the schematic with a whip stitch through back loops only.

Widening rows

Size 6 only
Using yarn A, work the widening rows on each section. With RS facing, join in the yarn at the point marked with a red cross on the schematic.

Row 1 (RS): 3 ch (counts as first tr), work 1 tr in each tr along, ending with 1 tr in final 2-ch sp, turn.
Rows 2 and 3 (WS): 3 ch, tr to end.
Fasten off.
Repeat on each section.

To finish

Join the squares as indicated on the schematic.

Join the fronts to the back noting that top square of the back joins to top front square and sits over the shoulder.

Armhole edging

Join yarn A at underarm.
Round 1 (RS): work 1 dc in each st and 1 dc in each join between squares around, sl st to join, turn.
Round 2 (WS): dc around, sl st to join.
Fasten off.

Use a brooch or a pin if you want to cinch the garment at the waist. You could also use a thin belt.

Bottom edging

Join yarn A at bottom of left front.

Row 1: 1 ch, work 1 dc in each dc or tr and 1 dc in each join between squares to bottom of right front, turn.

Row 2: 1 ch, dc to end, turn.

Sizes 5 and 6 only

Rows 3–6: 1 ch, dc to end, turn.
Fasten off.

Front edging

Join yarn A at bottom of right front under sc row end.

Row 1 (RS): 1 ch, work 1 dc in each dc row end, 1 dc in each st, and 1 dc in each join between squares to bottom of left front, turn.

Rows 2 and 3: 1 ch, dc to end, turn.
Fasten off.
Weave in all yarn ends.

Pair this maxi waistcoat with a billowy white blouse to add to the boho-chic look.

Everyday Long Cardigan

This gorgeous cardigan is perfect for everyday wear.
Jazz up a pair of jeans or pair with your favourite little dress.

Tools and materials

Scheepjes Softfun DK, 60% cotton, 40% acrylic
50g (1¾oz) = 140m (153yd)

Yarn A: Crepe 2612 x 6(7:9:11:13:14) balls

Yarn B: Denim 2489 x 1 ball

Yarn C: Light Blue 2432 x 1 ball

Yarn D: Peach 2466 x 1 balls

Yarn E: Bordeaux 2492 1 x 1 ball

Yarn F: Bumblebee 2634 x 1 ball

Yarn G: Tortilla 2632 x 2 balls

Yarn H: Periwinkle 2619 x 2 balls

Yarn I: Clay 2431 x 2 balls

Yarn J: Mustard 2621 x 2 balls

Yarn K: Lace 2426 x 3 balls

Size 4.5mm (7) hook

Yarn substitutes

Any DK weight yarn that works to the same tension would be a suitable substitute.

See also

• The classic granny square, page 14

Made with a combination yarn of cotton and acrylic, this cardigan is light, breathable and holds its shape well. Choose your palette well, and this cardigan could easily be your go-to cover-up for all your well-loved outfits.

Sizes and schematic

This garment is designed to be loose and roomy. Choose the size nearest to your actual chest measurement for a closer fit or go up a size or two for that oversized feel.

Size	1	2	3	4	5	6	
Actual chest	114	122	130	138	142	150	cm
	45	48	51¼	54⅜	56	59	in
Length	77	83	89	89	89	89	cm
	30¼	32¾	35	35	35	35	in
Sleeve length	27	29	31	31	31	31	cm
	10¾	11½	12¼	12¼	12¼	12¼	in

FRONT

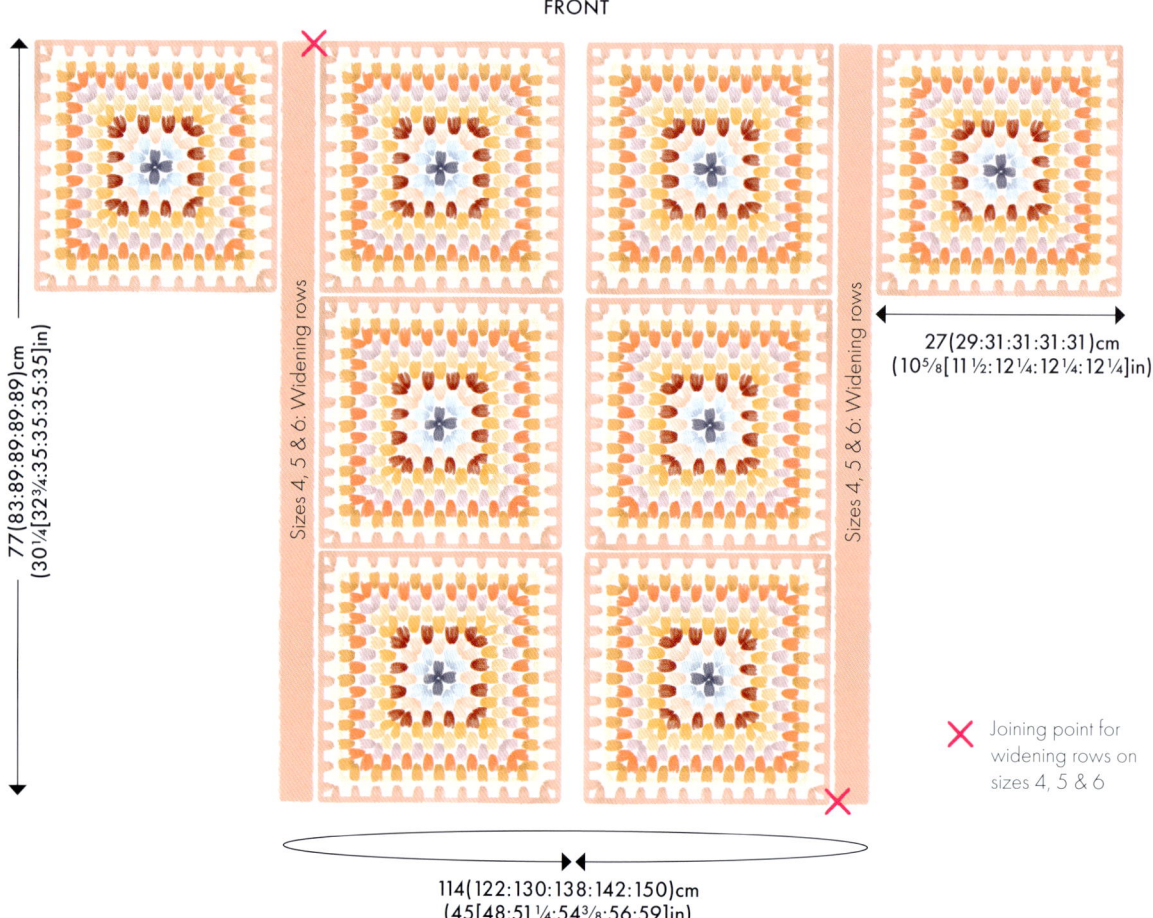

77(83:89:89:89:89)cm
(30¼[32¾:35:35:35:35]in)

Sizes 4, 5 & 6: Widening rows

Sizes 4, 5 & 6: Widening rows

27(29:31:31:31:31)cm
(10⅝[11½:12¼:12¼:12¼]in)

✕ Joining point for widening rows on sizes 4, 5 & 6

114(122:130:138:142:150)cm
(45[48:51¼:54⅜:56:59]in)

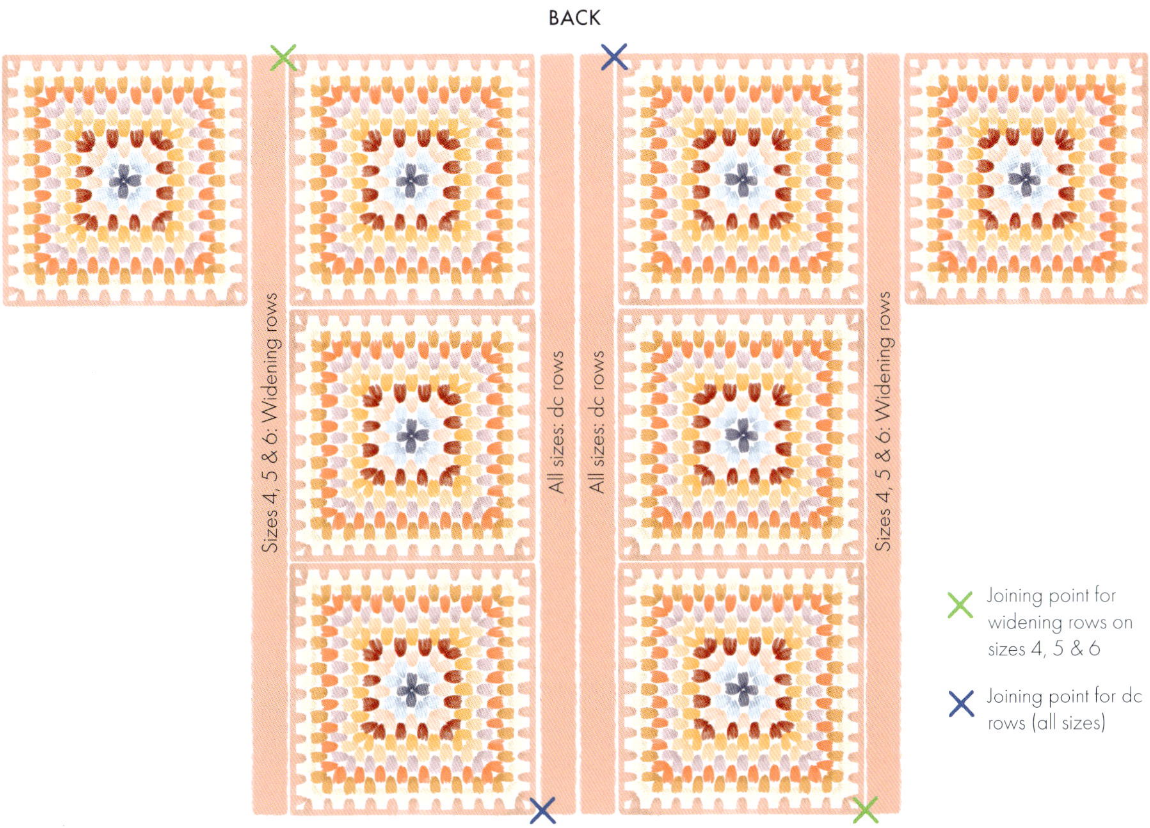

BACK

Sizes 4, 5 & 6: Widening rows

All sizes: dc rows

All sizes: dc rows

Sizes 4, 5 & 6: Widening rows

✕ Joining point for
widening rows on
sizes 4, 5 & 6

✕ Joining point for dc
rows (all sizes)

25(27:29:29:29:29)cm
(9¾ [10¾: 11 ½: 11 ½: 11 ½: 11 ½]in)

25(27:29:29:29:29)cm
(9¾ [10¾: 11 ½: 11 ½: 11 ½: 11 ½]in)

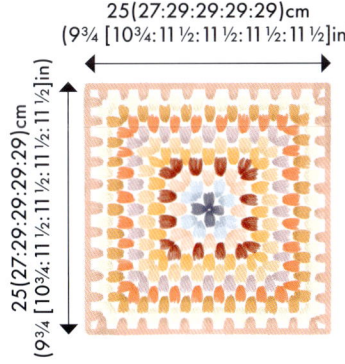

Tension

- Each square measures 25(27:29:29:29:29)
  x 25(27:29:29:29:29)cm
  (9¾[10¾: 11 ½: 11 ½: 11 ½: 11 ½] x
  9¾[10¾: 11 ½: 11 ½: 11 ½: 11 ½]in) using
  4.5mm (7) hook or size required to obtain
  tension.

Granny square (make 16)

Using yarn B, 4 ch, sl st to first ch to form ring.

Round 1 (RS): 3 ch (counts as tr here and throughout) 2 tr in ring, 2 ch, (3 tr, 2 ch) three times in ring, join with sl st to top of 3-ch, turn. Fasten off yarn B. Join yarn C in any 2-ch sp.

Round 2 (WS): 3 ch, (2 tr, 2 ch, 3 tr) in same 2-ch sp, (3 tr, 2 ch, 3 tr) in each of next three 2-ch sps, sl st to join, turn.
Fasten off yarn C. Join yarn D in any 2-ch sp.

Round 3 (RS): 3 ch, (2 tr, 2 ch, 3 tr) in same 2-ch sp, 3 tr in space before next 3-tr group, *(3 tr, 2 ch, 3 tr) in next 2-ch sp, 3 tr in space before next 3-tr group; rep from * twice more, sl st to top of beg 3-ch, turn.
Fasten off yarn D. Join yarn E in any 2-ch sp.

Round 4 (WS): 3 ch, (2 tr, 2 ch, 3 tr) in same 2-ch sp, 3 tr in space between each 3-tr group to corner 2-ch sp, *(3 tr, 2 ch, 3 tr) in next 2-ch sp, 3 tr in space between each 3-tr group to next corner 2-ch sp; rep from * twice more, sl st to top of beg 3-ch, turn.
Fasten off yarn E. Join yarn F in any 2-ch sp.

Round 5 (RS): as round 4.
Fasten off yarn F. Join yarn G in any 2-ch sp.

Round 6 (WS): as round 5.
Fasten off yarn G. Join yarn H in any 2-ch sp.

Round 7 (RS): as round 5.
Fasten off yarn H. Join yarn I in any 2-ch sp.

Round 8 (WS): as round 5.
Fasten off yarn I. Join yarn J in any 2-ch sp.

Round 9 (RS): as round 5.
Fasten off yarn J. Join yarn K in any 2-ch sp.

Round 10 (WS): as round 5.
Fasten off yarn K. Join yarn A in any 2-ch sp.

Round 11 (RS): as round 5.
Cont in yarn A only.

Sizes 2, 3, 4, 5 and 6 only

Round 12: sl st to first sp between tr, 3 ch, 2 tr in same space, 3 tr in space between each 3-tr group and (3 tr, 2 ch, 3 tr) in each corner 2-ch sp around, sl st to top of beg 3-ch.

Sizes 3, 4, 5 and 6 only

Round 13 (WS): as round 12.

Fasten off ALL SIZES.

This gorgeous cardigan reaches just above the knees. For a shorter, waist-length cardigan, remove the bottom set of squares (so you have 12 squares only).

To make up

Using a neat whip stitch, sew the squares together in sections as shown on the schematic.

With RS of back panel 1 facing, rejoin yarn A in corner ch sp as indicated by the red cross on schematic.

Row 1: 1 ch (does not count as a dc), 1 dc in each st and ch sp to end of row, turn.

Rows 2–5: 1 ch, dc to end, turn. Fasten off.

Repeat these 5 rows on back panel 2, joining the yarn in at the top left corner as indicated by the blue cross on the schematic.

Join both panels together down the centre back using a neat whip stitch.

To get a beautiful, seamless look, always use the main colour (yarn A) when joining the squares.

This everyday cardigan looks great paired with any colour from the square. Wear it with a yellow dress, as shown here, or something purple, maroon, orange, blue, beige or white. There are so many options!

Widening rows

Sizes 4, 5 and 6 only

With RS of the back facing, rejoin yarn A in corner 2-ch sp as indicated by the green cross on the schematic.

Row 1: 3 ch (counts as first tr), 1 tr in each tr to bottom of third granny square (do not work into ch sps at corners of squares), work 1 tr in bottom corner 2-ch sp, turn.

Row 2: 3 ch, tr to end.

Size 5 only

Rows 3–4: as row 2.

Size 6 only

Rows 3–6: as row 2.
Fasten off.

Repeat these rows on opposite side of the back panel, joining yarn A at the bottom right corner as indicated by the orange cross on the schematic.

Repeat for each front panel, joining yarn A at each corner marked with a pink cross.

Front edging

Worked in the same way on both sides of the front.

Rejoin yarn A in corner ch sp of bottom motif at opening edge of front panel.

Row 1: 1 ch, 1 dc in each st to end, turn.

Row 2: 1 ch, dc to end, turn.

Row 3: 1 ch, dc to end.
Fasten off.

Repeat on second front panel. Sew the front panels to the back at the shoulder, matching the side edge of the front to the widening rows on larger sizes.

Sleeves

Join two squares together with a whip stitch to make sleeve.

Cuff edging

With RS facing, rejoin yarn A at the underarm edge of the sleeve.

Round 1: 1 ch, work 1 dc in each st around, sl st to join, turn.

Round 2: 1 ch, dc around.
Fasten off.

Repeat on the second sleeve. Match the joining seam of the sleeve squares to the shoulder seam and sew the sleeves in place. Sew the side and sleeve seams.

Bottom edging

With RS of garment facing, hold the work upside down and rejoin yarn A to the bottom corner of left front.

Row 1: 1 ch, work 1 dc in each st, 1 dc under each dc row end and 2 dc under each tr row end around to bottom corner of right front, turn.

Row 2: 1 ch, dc to end, turn.
Fasten off.
Weave in all yarn ends.

CHAPTER THREE

Stitches and Techniques

From learning about hook sizes to taking care of finished pieces, this chapter will walk you through the essentials of crocheting. Basic stitches and useful techniques are covered with step-by-step instructions and illustrated with clear line drawings, so you can develop your skills and become a confident crocheter.

Yarn, Hooks and Materials

Yarn

Yarn is the generic term used to describe the material you crochet with. It can be a synthetic fibre such as acrylic, a natural fibre such as wool, or a blend of different fibres.

Yarn types

WOOL This is spun from sheep's fleece, so it is a natural fibre with a slight spring and is forgiving of mistakes. Some people have wool allergies, which is something to be aware of. It's a warmer choice and many of the projects in this book can be made with wool fibre for a warmer garment. Care will be needed when washing, as wool has a tendency to bobble or felt.

COTTON A natural fibre, cotton produces a durable fabric with gorgeous stitch definition and is naturally lightweight and breathable, making it perfect for summer outfits. As an inelastic fibre, it is a great choice for projects where you want the item to hold its shape.

ACRYLIC A man-made fibre, acrylic yarn is affordable and widely available. It is often combined with wool or cotton and can be a great budget choice for beginners or for larger items.

COMBINATION YARNS A yarn comprised of both wool and synthetic fibre is a dependable choice. Picking something that has a small percentage of synthetic fibre (for example, nylon or acrylic) makes a nice yarn to work with and launder.

Yarn weights

Yarn is generally categorized by the thickness of each strand, known as its weight. (Don't confuse this with the actual weight of the ball of yarn in grams or ounces.) The table below shows the most common weight categories and the names the yarns are usually known by, together with the tension range and hook sizes.

Yarn weight names	Tension range to 10cm (4in)	Hook size range
2-ply, fingering	32–42 dc	1.6–1.4mm (Steel 6–8); regular hook 2.25mm (B)
Sock, fingering, baby	21–32 dc	2.25–3.5mm (B–E)
4-ply, sport, baby	16–20 dc	3.5–4.5 mm (E–7)
DK, light worsted	12–17 dc	4.5–5.5mm (7–I)
Aran, worsted, afghan	11–14 dc	5.5–6.5mm (I–K)
Chunky, craft, rug	8–11 dc	6.5–9mm (K–M)
Super chunky, roving	7–9 dc	9–15mm (M–Q)

Ball bands

Most yarns come with a printed label that offers standard information on the fibre content, weight and aftercare. A standard ball band will provide the following information.

1 Name of yarn.
2 Yarn composition – which fibres have been used to make the yarn.
3 Weight of the ball – in grams and/or ounces.
4 Length of yarn – how many metres or yards are in the ball.
5 Recommended needle or hook size – usually given as a knitting needle size.
6 Tension – the number of stitches and rows you can expect over a 10cm (4in) square. Tension is usually given for a crocheted square, but the information can be useful if you are trying to substitute the yarn recommended in your pattern.
7 Aftercare and washing instructions – pay special attention to the washing instructions.
8 Colour shade name or number and dye lot – each batch of dye is given its own batch number and is produced in limited amounts. Because the shades can vary, always buy yarn with the same batch number if your pattern requires more than one ball.

Hooks

Crochet hooks come in different sizes and materials. To start out, it's best to use aluminium hooks, as they have a pointed head and well-defined throat and work well with most yarns. Bamboo hooks are also pleasing to work with, but can be slippery with some yarns. Plastic hooks can be squeaky with synthetic yarns. You can also purchase hooks with soft-grip or wooden handles, which make them more ergonomic.

What size hook?

You may find that using the hook size recommended for a particular yarn or pattern isn't satisfactory, and your work may be too tight or too loose. Try different hook sizes until it matches the designer's tension swatch. A tension square is essential to obtain the correct measurements when crocheting.

Materials

Although all you need to get started is a hook and some yarn, it's handy to have the following items in your work bag.

SCISSORS Use a pair of small, sharp embroidery scissors.

RULER AND MEASURING TAPE A rigid ruler is best for measuring tension. A sturdy measuring tape is good for taking larger measurements.

STITCH MARKERS Markers are handy for keeping track of the first stitch of a row or round, particularly when starting out. Also use them to hold the working loop when you put your work down for the night.

PINS Use rustproof, glass-headed pins for wet and steam blocking.

BLOCKING BOARDS Blocking boards are usually made of foam and are ideal for pinning out fabric. Some have a square grid that is helpful for pinning out shapes and squares with accuracy. You will find more information on blocking on page 137, so don't worry if you are unfamiliar with this term.

NEEDLES Yarn or tapestry needles are used for sewing seams together and weaving in yarn ends. Choose needles with blunt ends to avoid splitting stitches.

Starting and Finishing

Crochet can be worked in rows, beginning with a foundation chain, or in rounds, working outwards from a foundation ring of chain stitches or a magic ring.

Holding the hook and yarn

The two common ways of holding the hook, referred to as the pencil and knife hold, are shown here.

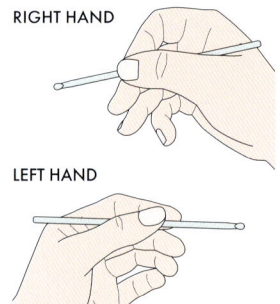

RIGHT HAND

LEFT HAND

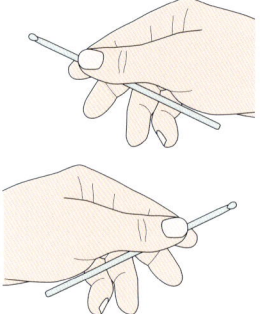

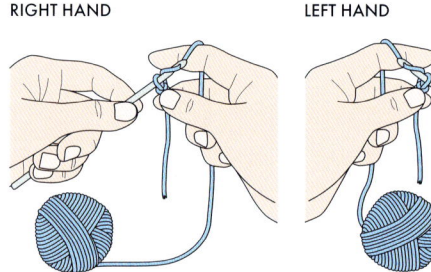

RIGHT HAND

LEFT HAND

Pencil hold
Centre the tips of your dominant thumb and forefinger over the flat section of the hook, as shown, as if you were holding a pen or pencil.

Knife hold
Grasp the flat section of the hook between your thumb and forefinger as if you were holding a knife.

Holding the yarn To control the supply and keep an even tension on the yarn, loop the short end of the yarn around your non-dominant forefinger, and take the yarn coming from the ball loosely around the little finger on the same hand. Use the middle finger on the same hand to help hold the work.

Foundation chain

The pattern will tell you how many chains to make. This may be a specific number or a multiple. If a pattern tells you to make a multiple of 3 + 2, this does not mean make a multiple of 5. It means that you should make a multiple of 3 and then add 2 chains—for example, 3 + 2, 6 + 2, 9 + 2 and so on. You may also be instructed to add a turning chain for the first row.

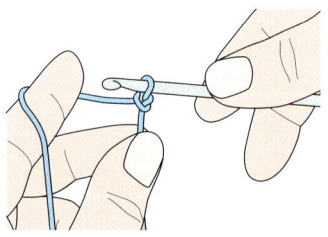

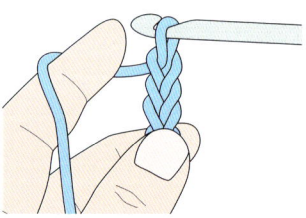

1 Holding the hook with the slip knot in your right hand and the yarn in your left hand, wrap the yarn around the hook. Draw the yarn through to make a new loop and complete the first chain stitch.

2 Repeat this process, drawing a new loop of yarn through the loop already on the hook until the chain is the required length. Count each V-shaped loop on the front of the chain as one chain stitch, except for the loop on the hook, which is not counted. After every few stitches, move up the thumb and finger that are grasping the chain to keep the chain stitches even.

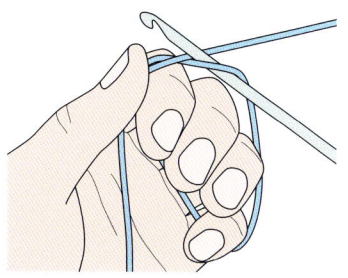
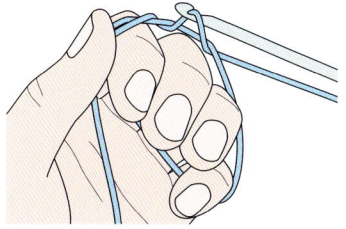

Making a slip knot

1 Loop the yarn as shown, insert the hook into the loop, catch the yarn with the hook and pull it through to make a loop over the hook.

2 Gently pull the yarn to tighten the loop around the hook.

3 Once tightened, the finished slip knot should sit just below the hook.

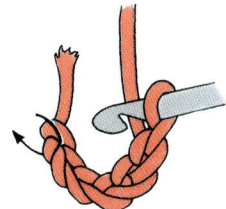
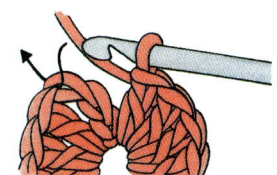
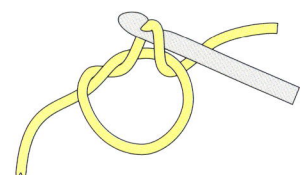

Foundation ring

1 Work a short length of chain as specified in the pattern. Join the chains into a ring by working a slip stitch (page 132) into the first chain of the foundation chain.

2 Work the first round of stitches into the centre of the ring unless specified otherwise. At the end of the round, the final stitch is usually joined to the first stitch with a slip stitch.

Magic ring

Use this alternative to a foundation ring for working in the round when you want to prevent a hole in the centre of your work. Wrap the yarn into a ring, insert the hook and draw a loop through. Work the first round of crochet stitches into this ring, then pull the yarn tail tightly to close the ring.

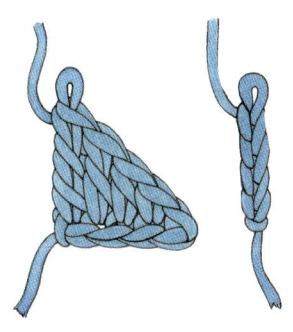

Turning and starting chains

When working crochet, you will need to work a specific number of extra chains at the beginning of each row or round. When the work is turned at the end of a straight row, the extra chains are called a turning chain, and when they are worked at the beginning of a round, they are called a starting chain. The extra chains bring the hook up to the correct height for the stitch you will be working next. The starting chain in the granny square is counted as the first stitch of the round. At the end of a round, the final stitch is usually joined to the starting chain with a slip stitch.

NUMBER OF TURNING CHAINS

Double crochet (dc): 1 turning chain
Half treble crochet (htr): 2 turning chains
Treble crochet (tr): 3 turning chains
Double treble crochet (dtr): 4 turning chains
Triple treble crochet (trtr): 5 turning chains
Quadruple treble crochet (qtr): 6 chains

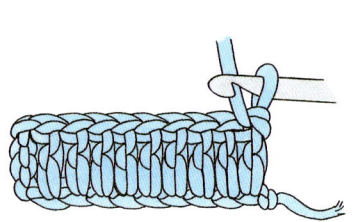

Fastening off

When you have completed your crochet, cut the yarn about 15cm (6in) from the last stitch. Wrap the yarn around the hook and draw the yarn end through the loop on the hook. Gently pull the yarn to tighten the last stitch, then weave in the yarn end.

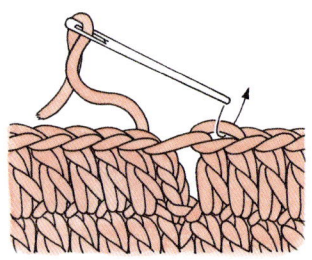

Finishing the last round

For a neater finish, don't use a slip stitch to join the last stitch of the final round to the first stitch of the round. Instead, fasten off the yarn after the last stitch, thread a yarn needle with the end of yarn, and pass it under the top loops of the first stitch of the round and back through the centre of the last stitch.

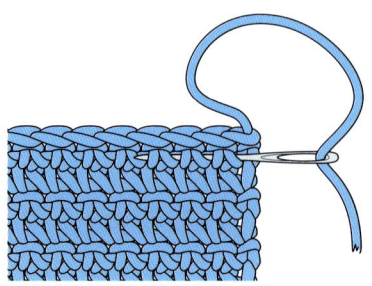

Weaving in ends

At the end of making your project, you will need to weave in any yarn ends from changing colours and sewing seams. For crochet worked in rows, use a yarn needle to sew in ends diagonally on the wrong side. For crochet worked in rounds, sew in ends under stitches for a few inches. If the pattern doesn't allow this, sew under a few stitches, then up through the back of a stitch and under a few more stitches on the next row.

Basic Stitches

All crochet stitches are based on a loop pulled through another loop by a hook. There are only a few stitches to master, each of a different length. Here is a concise guide to the basic stitches used to make the blocks.

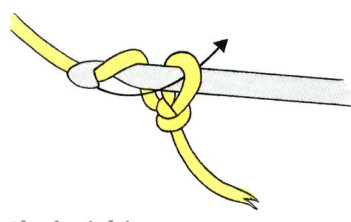

Chain (ch)

Wrap the yarn round the hook and pull it through the loop on the hook to form a new loop on the hook.

Slip stitch (sl st)

Insert the hook into the specified stitch, wrap the yarn round the hook and pull it through the stitch and the loop on the hook.

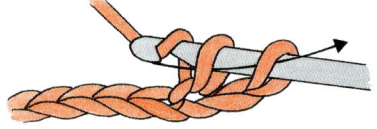

Double crochet (dc)

Insert the hook into the specified stitch, wrap the yarn round the hook and pull it through the stitch (2 loops on hook). Yarn round hook and pull it through both loops.

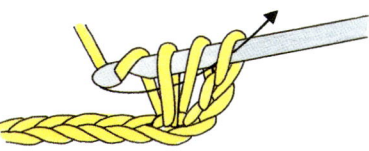

Half treble crochet (htr)

Yarn round hook, insert the hook into the specified stitch, yarn round hook and pull it through the stitch (3 loops on hook). Yarn round hook and pull it through all three loops.

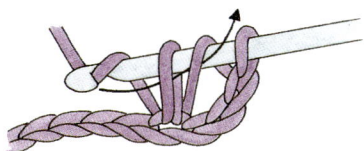

Treble crochet (tr)

Yarn round hook, insert the hook into the specified stitch, yarn round hook and pull it through the stitch (3 loops on hook). *Yarn round hook and pull it through two loops; repeat from * once more.

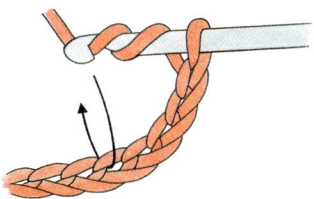

Double treble crochet (dtr)

Yarn round hook twice, insert the hook into the specified stitch, yarn round hook and pull it through the stitch (4 loops on hook). *Yarn round hook and pull it through two loops; repeat from * twice more.

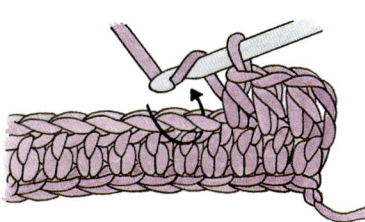

Through front loop only (FLO)

Rather than inserting the hook under both top loops to work the next stitch in the usual way, insert it only under the front loop.

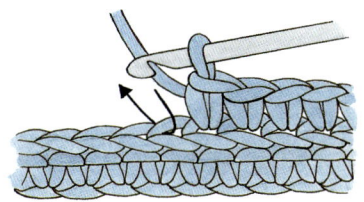

Through back loop only (BLO)

Rather than inserting the hook under both top loops to work the next stitch in the usual way, insert it only under the back loop.

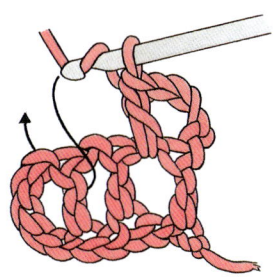

Into a chain space (ch sp)

Insert the hook into the space below a chain or chains. Here, a treble crochet is being worked into a chain space.

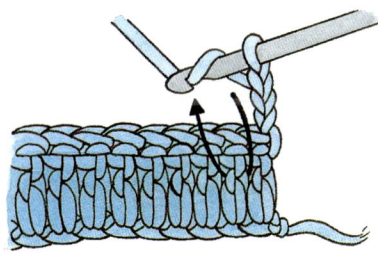

Around the front post (fp)

Work around the stem of the stitch, inserting the hook from front to back, around the post and to the front again.

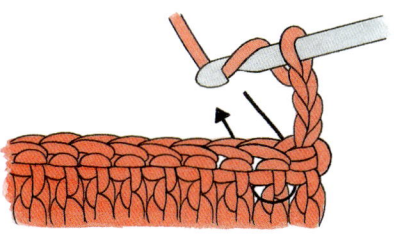

Around the back post (bp)

Work around the stem of the stitch, inserting the hook from back to front, around the post and to the back again.

MAKING TALLER STITCHES

You can make taller stitches by wrapping the yarn round the hook as many times as you wish before inserting the hook into the specified stitch. For example, wrap the yarn round the hook three times to make a triple treble crochet (trtr). Complete the stitch in the same way as double treble crochet, working off two loops at a time in the usual way.

Special Stitches

By working multiple stitches in the same place or working several stitches together at the top, or a combination of both, you can create interesting shapes, patterns and textures. The turning or starting chain may be counted as the first stitch of a special stitch.

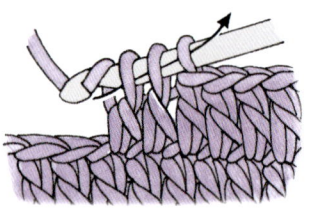

Decrease (e.g. tr2tog, dtr3tog)

One or two stitches can be decreased by working two or three incomplete stitches together. Work the specified number of stitches, omitting the final stage (the last yarn round hook) of each stitch so that the last loop of each stitch remains on the hook. Wrap the yarn round the hook and draw it through all the loops on the hook.

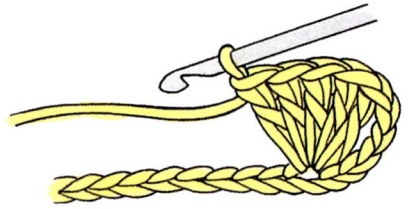

Increase (e.g. 5tr in next ch)

This technique is used to increase the total number of stitches when shaping an item, or to create a decorative effect such as a shell. Simply work the required number of stitches in the same place. Increases may be worked at the edges of flat pieces, or at any point along a row or round.

STAY STITCH

This is used on the rollneck of the Half & Half Jumper (page 72) to hold its rolled position. It is not necessary, but is easy to do. Simply place small straight stitches through both layers of the neck and fasten off tightly.

Reverse double crochet

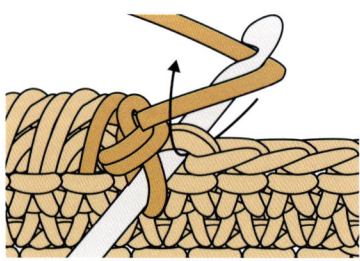

1 Insert the hook into the top of the previous stitch (without turning your work). This will be to the right for right-handed, or to the left for left-handed crocheters. Wrap the yarn round the hook.

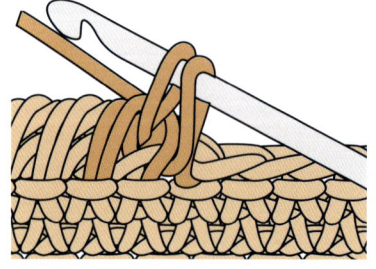

2 Pull the yarn through the stitch to make two loops on the hook.

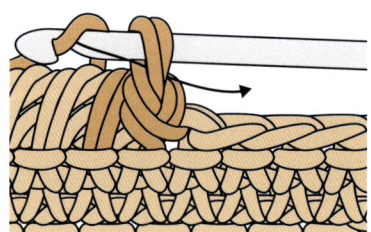

3 Wrap the yarn round the hook again and pull it through both loops on the hook. One reverse double crochet stitch made.

Colourwork

There are several ways to change colours on each round of the square. The simplest is to use a slip stitch join, but you can try another technique known as the tie-in method.

Tie-in method

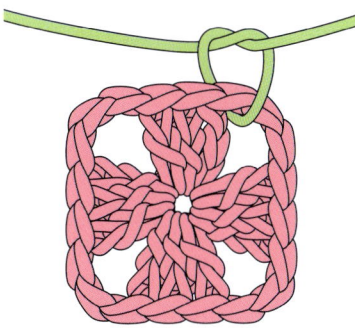

1 Join the new yarn to any chain space by slipping the tail of the yarn through the chain space and tying it in a knot, leaving a 5cm (2in) tail (this can be woven in later).

2 Insert the hook from front to back into the chain space, pick up the working yarn and make the number of starting chains specified in the pattern.

Joining in with a slip stitch

You can also join a new yarn using a slip stitch. This can be used with any of the basic stitches; here it is shown using treble crochet. It is best to join the new yarn at the beginning of the row.

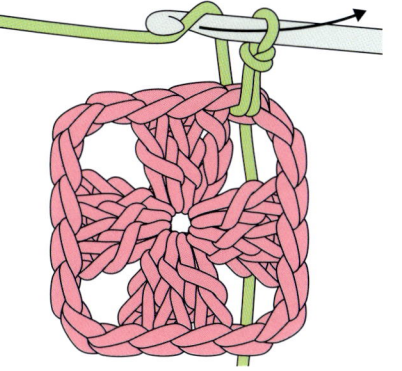

1 Make a slip knot in the new yarn. Insert the hook from front to back through the first crochet stitch of the row and then pick up the slip knot.

2 Pull the slip knot through the stitch. Wrap the yarn over the hook and draw it through the slip knot to secure the yarn and make the first turning chain. Make two more turning chains (or the number required for the stitch you are working).

CREATING A COLOUR PALETTE

You can either follow the suggestions in this book or choose you own. Colours are the most important element of your project, but how do you pick the right palette? There is no golden rule or big secret to picking a perfect palette for your project. There are no 'wrong' colours. Before setting foot in the yarn store with the intention to buy, spend some time working out the colour combinations you are drawn to. Once you have a collection of yarns to work with, try adding new colours and taking colours away. Play around for as long as necessary to get a selection you are happy with.

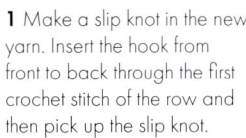

Joining

Squares can be joined by sewing or by crochet. Pin seams together to help match up the blocks and give a neat finish. Use the same yarn that you used for the blocks, or a finer yarn, preferably with the same fibre content.

Join as you go

This simple method is sometimes called a flat join because the resulting join is a smooth and unobtrusive flat seam.

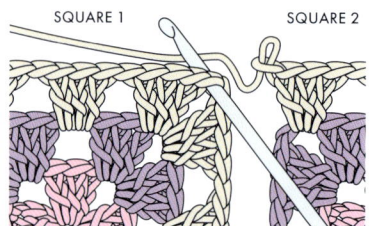

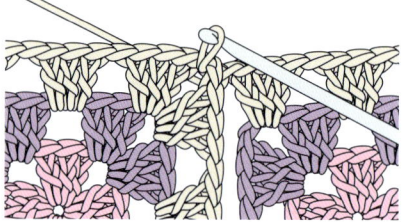

1 Complete the first square and then work the second square as far as the final round.

2 Join the yarn for the final round into any corner chain space of the second square. Work the first side of the square as usual as far as the second corner.

3 Work the second corner up to the halfway point – here, 3 tr, 1 ch. Remove the hook from the working loop, then insert the hook from front to back into any corner chain space on the first square.

4 Put the working loop back on the hook and draw the loop through the corner chain space of the first square to the front. Complete the corner by working 1 ch, 3 tr. The two squares are now joined at the corner.

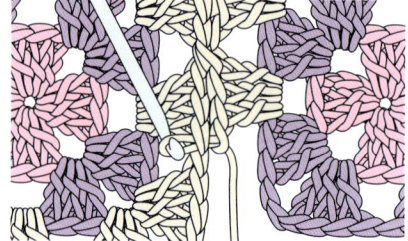

Whip stitch

Sometimes called oversewing or overcast stitch, this is more flexible than backstitch. It is very popular with crochet designers and experienced crocheters because it creates an almost invisible seam.

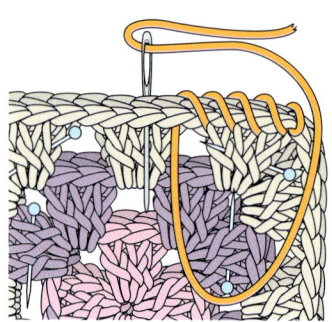

Pin the pieces to be joined together, as for backstitch. Working from right to left, take the needle over the edge of the work and then bring it from back to front through both layers of fabric. Make each stitch slightly in front of the previous stitch.

5 Continue to work the final round of the second square, joining the squares at each space between a 3-tr group along the side edge in the same way as at the corner.

6 When you reach the next corner, join the two squares as before and then complete the final round of the second square. The two squares are now joined together along one side.

7 To make a strip of squares, simply carry on joining further squares in the same way, joining them at two corners and along one side edge.

Tension and Blocking

It's important to crochet a test swatch before you start your project to establish tension. To finish off your block neatly, you will need to block it. You can use the tension swatch to test blocking and cleaning methods.

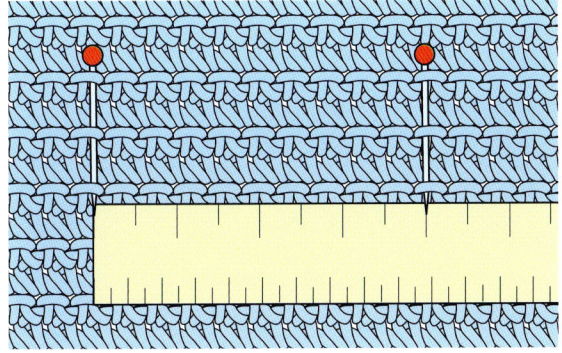

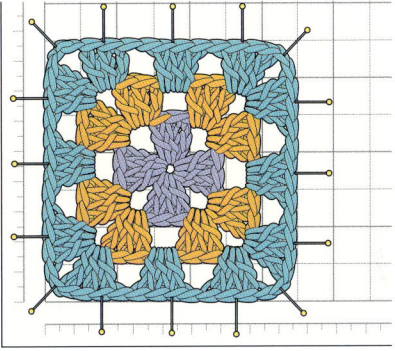

Measuring tension

No two people will crochet to the exact same tension, even when working with identical yarn and hooks. Always make a test swatch or square before starting a project so that you can compare your tension with the pattern tension and get an idea of how the finished project will feel and drape. It's also useful for testing out different colour combinations.

To test your tension, make a sample swatch or square in the yarn you intend to use following the pattern directions. Block the sample and then measure again. If your sample is larger, try making another using a smaller hook. If your sample is smaller, try making another using a bigger hook. Also do this if the fabric feels too loose and floppy or too dense and rigid. Keep trying until you find a hook size that will give you the required tension, or until you are happy with the drape and feel of your work. Ultimately, it's more important that you use a hook and yarn you are comfortable with than that you rigidly follow the pattern instructions.

Blocking

Blocking is crucial to set the stitches and even out the piece. Choose a method based on the care label of the yarn. When in doubt, use the wet method. Use an ironing board or a foam block, or make a blocking board by securing one or two layers of quilter's wadding, covered with a sheet of cotton fabric, over a flat board.

WET METHOD – ACRYLIC AND WOOL/ACRYLIC MIX

Using rustproof pins, pin the crochet fabric to the correct measurements on a flat surface and dampen using a spray bottle of cold water. Pat the fabric to help the moisture penetrate. Ease stitches into position, keeping rows and stitches straight. Allow to dry before removing the pins.

STEAM METHOD – WOOLS AND COTTONS

Pin out the fabric as above. For fabric with raised stitches, pin it right side up to avoid squashing the stitches; otherwise, pin it wrong side up. Steam lightly, holding the iron 2.5cm (1in) above the fabric. Allow the steam to penetrate for several seconds. It is safer to avoid pressing, but if you choose to do so, cover with a clean towel or cloth first.

Crocheting Clothes

Crocheting your own clothes means that each piece is one-of-a-kind and that you'll have a lower environmental impact by not supporting fast fashion. It can also be therapeutic; working with your hands is incredibly relaxing and the final result will be a culmination of your hard work which you can show off at home, school or at work.

Washing and storage

It is a good idea to keep a ball band from each project you complete as a reference for washing instructions. Crochet items are best washed gently by hand and dried flat on a towel to keep their shape. Do not hang, as the weight of the water will stretch the item. If the yarn you have used is machine washable, put the item into a zipped mesh laundry bag to prevent it from stretching and snagging during the wash cycle. Crochet garments should not be hung on coat hangers, but folded and stored flat, away from dust, damp, heat and sunlight. Clean tissue paper is better than a plastic bag.

Note: Crochet clothing may not need to be washed after every use, especially if it's a jumper or a poncho that's layered with other clothing. Try spraying with a fabric refresher for a quick freshen up.

Project notes

When you have finished making a crochet project, store a small amount of leftover yarn from each project in case you need to make future repairs. Punch a hole in a piece of card and knot several lengths of yarn through the hole. Make a note of the type of yarn and colour, as well as details of the project, and attach one of the ball bands to remind you of the yarn composition and any special pressing or washing instructions.

PURE WOOL

Pure wool must be washed by hand in cold water to avoid felting and shrinking. Choose a detergent formula developed for wool or a mild baby shampoo.

TREATING STAINS

Most stains can be removed by treating the area with a dab of heavy-duty detergent. Work the detergent into the yarn with your fingers, and allow it to sit for 15 minutes before washing.

FIXING PROBLEMS

Crochet items can be challenging to repair. Small holes can be tightened by hand-stitching with matching colour yarn or threads. However, if the break is significant, there may be nothing you can do other than unravelling the problematic square and crocheting again.

Understanding sizing

On each pattern within the book, you will find a table of all sizes, and the important measurements. The different sizes may mean either you need to create a larger square or more squares. The illustrated tension swatch corresponds with the sizing chart and you should follow the set of numbers that corresponds with each size as follows 1(2:3:4:5:6) and so on. Using the example square on the right, you would need to crochet a square 15 x 15cm (6 x 6in) for size 2 and 18 x 18cm (7 x 7in) for a size 6.

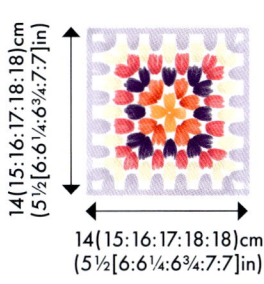

14(15:16:17:18:18)cm
(5½[6:6¼:6¾:7:7]in)

Measuring yourself

These are the most important measurements to know for the patterns in this book. Make a note of the following:

1. Chest/bust circumference
2. Armhole circumference
3. Waist circumference
4. Arm length to shoulder
5. Sleeve length
6. Upper arm circumference

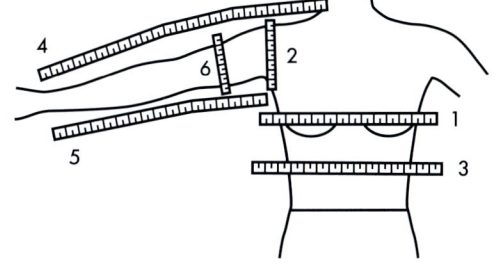

Accurate body measurements are vital but the fit of a finished item can vary from the actual body measurements by an extra 15cm (6in) or more. This difference is known as ease. By knowing your body measurements you're one step closer to deciding what type of ease you want. Some patterns might be designed to fit loosely.

USE YOUR WARDROBE

1 Go to your wardrobe and grab a garment you like that is similar to the one you're going to crochet.

2 Measure that garment the same way you did on your body earlier.

By knowing the difference between your body measurements and the measurements for your favourite garment, you are better equipped to choose the right size to crochet.

Yarn quantities

For different sizes, you may need more skeins or balls of yarn. This is indicated in brackets in the tools and materials of the pattern like so:

Yarn A: Orchid 2657 x 6(7:8:9:11:12) balls

This means that size 1 will need 6 balls of Yarn A. Size 2 will need 7 balls, size 3 will need 9 balls, and so on. If there are no brackets, then the quantity of balls does not change for the different sizes.

Yarn choice

Consider your yarn choice carefully, as it takes many hours to crochet a garment. You don't want a crochet garment that you can't or won't use. You can learn more about the different yarns on page 128. The easiest choice, of course, is to use the exact yarn suggested for the pattern. In that way, you also don't have to spend too much time checking the tension.

Reading Patterns and Charts

Below is a list of the crochet abbreviations and symbols used in this book. Please note that abbreviations and symbols may vary from one pattern publisher to another, so always read the list provided with the pattern you are using before starting a project.

Symbols

Symbol	Abbreviation	Description
⌒	ch	chain
•	sl st	slip stitch
+	dc	double crochet
T	htr	half treble crochet
⊤	tr	treble crochet
⊤	dtr	double treble crochet
⊤	trtr	triple treble crochet
⋀	cl	cluster (e.g. cluster of 4 tr)
⌢	blo	back loop only (e.g. dc blo)
⌣	flo	front loop only (e.g. dc flo)
ↄ	FP	front post (e.g. FPtr)
ↄ	BP	back post (e.g. BPtr)
►		beginning of row or round
≁	rdc	reverse double crochet
✿		4ch and sl st in first ch to form a ring.

Common Stitches (UK/US)

Some American terms differ from the English system, as shown below. Patterns you may encounter that are published using American terminology can be very confusing unless you understand the difference.

Symbol	English	American
+	double crochet (dc)	single crochet (sc)
T	half treble (htr)	half double (hdc)
⊤	treble (tr)	double (dc)
⊤	double treble (dtr)	treble (tr)
⊤	triple treble (ttr)	double treble (dtr)

Abbreviations

beg	beginning
rep	repeat
RS	right side
sp	space
st(s)	stitch(es)
tog	together
WS	wrong side
yo/yrh	yarn over/yarn round hook

Example chart

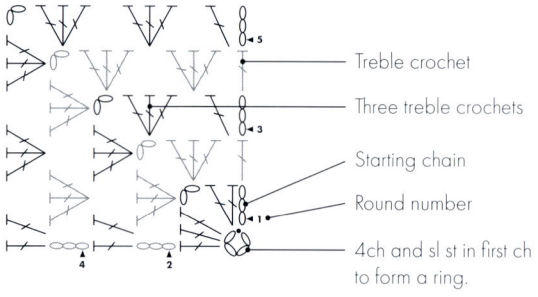

- Treble crochet
- Three treble crochets
- Starting chain
- Round number
- 4ch and sl st in first ch to form a ring.

Arrangement of symbols

JOINED AT TOP

A group of symbols joined at the top indicates that these stitches should be worked together at the top, as in cluster stitches, and for decreasing the number of stitches (for example, tr3tog or 4-tr cluster).

JOINED AT BASE

Symbols joined at the base should all be worked into the same stitch below (for example, 2 dc in same place or 5-tr shell).

General instructions

*   Start of repeat

* *   End of last repeat

[ ]   Repeat instructions within brackets the stated number of times

( )   Can either be explanatory (counts as 1 tr) or can be read as a group of stitches worked into the same stitch or space (1 tr, ch 2, 1 tr). For patterns with different sizes, the number of repeats required may differ. This is indicated like so: **-(-:-:-:- :1:2:3:4) times**. The dashes mean no repeats are required for sizes 1-5, but it needs to be repeated once for size 6, twice for size 7 and so on.

Reading charts

CHARTS IN ROWS

- Right-side rows start at the right, and are read from right to left.
- Wrong-side rows start at the left, and are read from left to right.

CHARTS IN ROUNDS

These charts begin at the centre, and each round is read anticlockwise, in the same direction as working. Occasionally, a block worked in the round may require you to turn the work, indicated by an arrow on the chart, in which case the round should be read in the direction of the arrow.

Glossary

BLOCK A square, hexagon or other regular shape, worked either in rows or in the round, designed to be repeated and joined together like fabric patchwork. Also known as a motif or medallion.

BLOCKING Setting a piece of crochet by pinning it out on a flat surface, either wetting it beforehand or spraying or steaming it afterwards, and then allowing to dry.

CHAIN SPACE The space below chain stitches.

CLUSTER Several incomplete stitches worked together so that they join at the top.

EDGING A decorative trim applied to the edges of crochet or woven fabric. Edgings can be worked separately and sewn on, or they can be worked directly onto the fabric.

FOUNDATION CHAIN A length of chain stitches that forms the base for a piece of crochet.

FOUNDATION ROW A technique for working the first row of crochet without a foundation chain. Some designers also use the term to refer to the first row worked into the foundation chain when that row will not be repeated as part of the stitch pattern.

TENSION The number of stitches and rows to a given measurement, usually 10cm (4in) square, with a suggested hook size.

MOTIF Another name for a block, but most commonly worked in the round. Motifs can be regular or irregular in shape.

MULTIPLE The number of chains to make for the foundation chain expressed as a multiple of a specific number; this allows the design to be scaled up or down as required. A specified number of extra chains is often added after the multiple calculation to allow for the turning chain and/or to balance the design.

STARTING CHAIN The name for a turning chain when working in the round.

TURNING CHAIN A number of chains worked at the beginning of a row to bring the hook up to the correct height for the next stitch that is being worked.

YARN ROUND HOOK Yarn wrapped around the hook.

Index

Projects are in **bold** type.

Credits

Author's Acknowledgements

Creating this book has been an absolute dream come true. I would not have been able to do it without the absolutely amazing team behind me and the support of my family, especially my gorgeous boys Harvey and Alfie, who have to put up with the extra balls of wool round the house and occasional takeaway dinner.

Special mention must go to Charlene, Martina, Sally and the whole team at Quarto for their belief in me and for allowing me to create a book that really encompasses my passion for granny squares.

Charlene was so amazing at making the whole process go smoothly.

Thank you to my tech editor and my now friend Rachel Vowles, without her I don't know what I would do.

Thank you to Claire Montgomerie; I was so grateful you were able to style the projects so beautifully. Having worked together for 15 years freelance, there really was no one else I'd rather ask.

Thank you to the superb Leanne Jade Photography. Your excellent personality always puts the models at ease and you always manage to capture the best shots and really make sure the models have the best day.

Thank you to my make-up artist Julia Edwards who ensured all the models looked absolutely stunning across the two days.

Thank you to all the models (Hattie, Sunny, Starlin and Chris) – you were an absolute joy to work with. It was also a great pleasure to be able to invite my friend Louise Willis to model and to share some of the journey with her. Thanks, Lou.

Thank you to my mate Felicity – your constant cheerleading and lengthy phone calls are part of the reason this book has made it to publication.

Thank you also to my partner Cliff, who has to share his time with me with a crochet hook and a few balls of wool!

Thanks to my dad who, up until his passing in March 2023, shared every post, and told every person he met about me being a designer. He wore my crocheted garments and he would have loved to have seen my work in print; thanks for being my rock.

Thank you to each and every person who has supported me along the way; every Instagram like, 'Well Done', or 'I love that' has given me the confidence to pursue a career I could only ever have dreamed of a few years ago.

Quarto would like to thank Scheepjes® for supplying all the yarn used in this book. For a full list of yarns available, please visit their website: www.scheepjes.com You can also find them on Instagram @scheepjes.